DR. CASSUNDRA WHITE-ELLIOTT

THE LAST
SHALL BE
FIRST

AN ANALYSIS OF THE
SYSTEMIC SUBDIVIDE
OF BLACK AMERICA

CLF Publishing, LLC.
www.clfpublishing.org
(909) 315-3161

Cover design by Senir Design. Contact information: info@senirdesign.com.

ISBN #978-1-945102-62-2

Printed in the United States of America.

Dedications

This book is dedicated to all of my brothers and sisters who share a heritage, a lineage, a race, and a culture with me. Those who have suffered alongside me in this land of opportunity, this land of the free. Those who have felt the stinging darts of racism, discrimination, and hatred directed towards them, their parents, grandparents, and their children. For those who know the struggle is yet alive and that the war rages on.

The Appeal:

Share this book with everyone you know. Tell them where to obtain their personal copy; then, ask them to tell others within their circle. I was mandated by Holy Spirit to write. And with the pen of a ready writer, I composed this book with the guidance of Holy Spirit. You are mandated to read and to spread the word. Just like anything else on social media, let this book spread like wildfire. Let it go viral and spread to the masses. This book is not limited to being read by just a few, but by all Black Americans, rich or poor, educated and uneducated, in the inner city or in the suburbs, believer and non-believer.

Acknowledgements

For my friends who listened as I shared what the Lord
gave to me for all of us.

Table of Contents

Introduction

The difficult and heart-wrenching instances of discrimination, racism, inequity, and inequality people of color experience can seem unbearable and everlasting. However, imbedded in God's Word, we find hope for a better tomorrow. God's Word shines light at the end of the metaphorical tunnel, showing us a way out of a chaotic life filled with challenges. Psalm 30:5b (KJV) says, *"weeping may endure for a night, but joy* cometh *in the morning."* What message does this verse convey? It tells us the times of sorrow will not last always. Over time, by God's grace, joy will spring eternal and replace the heartache, even the heartache that is seemingly never ending.

In due season, if we do not faint, we will reap God's benefits (Galatians 6:9). When His hand begins to move on our behalf, we **will** see a better tomorrow. But until a better tomorrow rests on the horizon, we must keep the faith. We must be steadfast and always abounding in good works. It will be the good works that will effectuate the must-needed change in our circumstances. Therefore, we must find ourselves being agents of change rather than agents of complacency, settling for the status quo and sitting in the shadows, while complaining about the lack of change.

God has already given us the power, the authority, and the ability to cause change to be manifested in our own lives. Luke 10:19 (KJV) says, *"Behold, I give unto you power to tread on serpents and scorpions, and over all the power of the enemy: and nothing shall by any means hurt you."* According to Barnes Notes on the Bible, "the enemy" does not <u>only</u> refer to Satan but also to his emissaries- all wicked and crafty men, men who practice presenting ill will to those unlike himself as if though he is a superior being.

With our God-given power, we can change our current situation. God has brought us this far along the way, and He will not fail us now. God loves us, and it should go without saying that He wants the best for us. The Word of God tells us in Job 8:7 (ISV), *"Your beginning may be small, but later years will be very great."* And because the Word of God is more powerful and sharper than a two-edged sword (Hebrews 4:12), we would do well to hold to His promises, knowing that His words will not return unto Him void but will accomplish that for which they have been sent (Isaiah 55:11).

In the midst of trying to understand the messages God has sent to us in this season (which will be detailed in the coming chapters of the book), we must hold tight to two verses: Hosea 4:6: *"My people are destroyed for lack of knowledge"* (KJV) and II Chronicles 7:14: *"If My people who are called by My name will humble themselves, and pray and seek My face, and turn from their wicked ways, then I will hear from heaven, and will forgive their sin and heal their land"* (NKJV).

First, in order to effectuate change, we must attend to Hosea 4:6, which informs us of the result of lacking knowledge, for our possession of it is necessary to initiate change. On the other hand, the lack of knowledge will lead us directly toward and into destruction. In the case of "moving forward" and away from the heart-wrenching experiences of racism, discrimination, ill treatment, inequalities, and inequities, we must have knowledge about the past. Although we do not dwell on the past as Apostle Paul instructs us in Philippians 3:13-14, there is one thing about the past we should definitely know: Events, practices, and circumstances have a way of circling around throughout history.

Ecclesiastes 1:9 (NKJV) informs us, *"That which has been is what will be, That which is done is what will be done, And there is nothing new under the sun."* Simply put, what has happened before will undoubtedly occur again. Therefore, we should be prepared, so we are not caught off guard when the enemy's snares present themselves. We will read more about this in the coming chapters.

Secondly, we must examine ourselves, according to II Chronicles 7:14, to see if there are any errors in our ways (behaviors, attitudes, mindsets, thoughts, deeds) and if so, we must admit our faults and be willing to change for the betterment of ourselves, our families, our community, and our "nation" (not the nation of the United States, but the "nation" of Black Americans). Without a willingness to conduct a self-examination and a willingness for positive change, we will forever be stagnated in a never-ending cycle of despair, finding ourselves with no hope, no will, and no advancement.

It is easy to point our fingers at others and play the fault-finding game, and, yes, others are definitely at fault for the substandard existence (comparatively speaking) that Blacks have had and continue to endure. But the question becomes, "Do others bear the burden of fault alone?" If we would dare to tell the truth and face it straight on, we will realize that we must own the errors that we ourselves have committed. In doing so, we will know where corrections must be made in order to effectuate change.

In an attempt to fully exemplify what God has in store for Black Americans and the meaning of the words *"The Last Shall be First,"* I must take you on a journey back in history to the 13th or 14th century B.C. (The exact time frame has not been determined by theologians.) According to the Holy Writ in the book of Exodus, it was during that time that the great Exodus occurred, which was the liberation of the people of Israel from slavery in Egypt. Under the leadership of Moses (and subsequently by Joshua), the Israelites were led into the Promised Land, a land the Lord described as one flowing with milk and honey. In modern day language, milk and honey is equivalent to prosperity. In the

Promised Land, the Israelites would experience freedom from bondage, oppression, and the heavy hand of slavery. They could relish in all the freedoms the Lord had in store for them.

After a brief trip to the B.C. era to survey the Israelites' plight, we will take a great leap in time, moving forward to the 16th century A.D. to examine the Trans-Atlantic Slave Trade of Africans and the plight of African slaves and how the slave trade and the imbedded conditions served as an impetus for the mistreatment of all descendants of Africa along with other Black Americans whose heritage is rooted in places such as the Caribbean.

After close examination of each event, a correlation can be drawn between these two historical events (the Exodus and the Trans-Atlantic Slave Trade). The correlation will serve to exemplify what the Lord wants to do during this day and age of unrest and turmoil that lies amidst systemic racism, discrimination, and degradation. Then, we will conduct an examination of specific conditions that must exist for Black Americans (as a whole) in order to tap into the blessings God has in store for us.

Chapters Five and Six will explain the wealth transfer that has already begun to take place in the earth realm and bring all discussed topics together into one conversation, bringing clarity to all examined subject matter.

Before delving into the deep waters of the subject matter, allow me to whisper a prayer.

It is my prayer, Lord Father, that after your people read this book, they will rise up and call your name blessed.
They will adhere to your words!
They will answer the clarion call!
And, they will receive all that you have in store for them!

Lord God, I thank you for the blessings that you have poured out and will continue to pour out. It is past time for a change, and I declare and decree that change will be manifested now, in the name of Jesus the Christ, our Lord and our Savior!

I pray that your boldness will infiltrate not only the spirits of your people but their minds as well. God, allow their anger to be healthy anger rather than destructive anger, motivating them to have a deep desire for permanent change that is long overdue.

Father, I thank you for all the blessings you have in store for us and the blessings you have already begun to pour out. Lord, you are so good to us, and we thank you. We bless your name God, for showing yourself strong and mighty and that you truly are the Alpha and the Omega. You had the first word, and you will have the last word. Lord God, we are standing on your promises. And, I ask you to order our steps and make every crooked path straight.

I thank you for being Jehovah Jirah, the God who provides, the God who will see to it. Your Word tells us that our latter days will be greater than the rest. Your Word tells us that the last will be first, and we receive your promises, knowing that you have not forgotten about us. Lord, let your love and favor pour out upon us. Guide us into all righteousness. Soften the hearts of those who stand against us, putting up road blocks to impede our progress. No longer will we stand being unheard and unseen by the masses. The time is long overdue for a change, and we thank you, Lord that the time is nigh. We thank you that real change is coming!

We thank you, Lord, and we honor you, as you pour out your wisdom upon us, showing us the way to go and for giving us the resources to carry out this great commission. Lord, on bended knees, we thank you!

Father God, I submit this petition in the name of our savior, Jesus. Amen!

Hallelulah!

To God be all the glory that is due unto His High and Holy name.

May the Lord forever be praised.

Chapter One
The Great Exodus

Between the covers of God's Holy Word, many men's and women's lives are detailed, providing us with information about God's essence and His love for mankind, His creation. From Genesis to Revelation, we learn of God's handiwork, exemplifying the power and authority that help define God's character. Surveying a person's life's work, walk of obedience to God's instruction, and the impact the work had on the outcome of God's plan provides a backdrop and lays a blueprint for a call to action that will be manifested for others throughout the course of history. Of all the men and women portrayed in the Bible, there is one specific person whose hand was directly involved in God's plan for His chosen people. In this chapter, a review of the life of Moses, a servant of God, will be presented. Let's see what helpful tips we can extrapolate which may be useful for the call to action that lies ahead of us.

At the time of Moses' birth, a decree had been issued by the king, mandating all newborn Hebrew boys be slain. The fact that the Hebrew people had already begun to outnumber the Egyptians and had begun to be seen as a possible physical threat was the catalyst for the decree. The mandate was the king's method of ensuring population control and hence the Egyptians' safety. In light of the decree and after having given birth to a baby boy, Moses' mother did her best to keep Moses hidden, attempting to save his life and to give him a future. When Moses was a few months of age, his mother placed him in a basket and set the basket upon the Nile river. Moses' older sister Miriam was tasked to watch over the basket as the current moved it along.

Eventually, the basket landed in the hands of Pharaoh's daughter. The princess ordered her servant to remove the basket from the river, revealing a baby boy. The princess realized he was a Hebrew child but did not order him to be slain. Miriam, not far away, asked the princess if she wanted Miriam to ask one of the Hebrew women to nurse the baby for her. The princess consented, and Miriam returned Moses back to their mother.

Moses remained in his mother's custody until he was weaned from her breastmilk. Then, he was returned to Pharaoh's daughter to be raised as her own son. From that point forward, Moses was raised as no other Hebrew could ever expect to live under their current living conditions. Unlike his Hebrew relatives, Moses wore the finest clothes and ate the best foods. But, life as Moses had grown accustomed would forever change, and his life would begin to charter a different course.

One day, Moses ventured out from the palace to see his own people. During his excursion, he witnessed an Egyptian task-master beating a Hebrew slave. Horrified by the treatment of his own people, Moses intervened and killed the Egyptian. The next day, Moses went out from the palace once again. Unfortunately, another disturbing scene awaited him. That time, he witnessed two Hebrew men fighting with one another. When Moses attempted to intervene and squash the dispute, one of the men asked who Moses thought he was to intervene in their affair. The man asked Moses if he were their judge and jury and if he would slay him as he had slain the Egyptian the day before.

Before slaying the Egyptian the day before, Moses had surveyed the area to see if any witnesses were present. Although he had not seen any, hearing the Hebrew's question, Moses was suddenly aware that the deed he had committed was not a secret as he had believed. His actions had become known and had even made it to the ears of Pharaoh. From that moment, Pharaoh sought to kill Moses even though Moses had been raised in his home.

Being startled to his core and fearing for his life, Moses fled Egypt without taking a look behind him. Looking for the shelter of safety, Moses kept running until he landed in Midian, which is on the opposite side of Mount Sinai, also known as Mount Horeb. Mount Sinai is a mountain that separates Egypt and Midian. Having found a safe place to dwell, Moses soon met Jethro and his daughters. Not long after, Moses married Zipporah, one of Jethro's daughters, and they had two sons. For the next forty years, Moses lived as a shepherd with his family. But, once again, something unexpected would occur, and Moses' life would once again be set on an alternate trajectory.

It is very interesting to us how our life seemingly changes course when an unexpected event occurs. In our mind, the event happened without just cause, and suddenly, we are on a different path. That ideal is far from reality. Jeremiah 1:5 (NKJV) says, *"Before I formed you in the womb I knew you; Before you were born I sanctified you; I ordained you a prophet to the nations."* That was the word given to the prophet Jeremiah, and the same is true for us. God knew us and the designated purpose He had for us before we were born. Therefore, we must understand and remember: Nothing happens to us by accident. God has our course already chartered.

Philippians 1:6 (NIV) says, *"being confident of this, that he who began a good work in you will carry it on to completion until the day of Christ Jesus."* And, Psalm 138:8 (NLT) says, *"The LORD will work out his plans for my life— for your faithful love, O LORD, endures forever. Don't abandon me, for you made me."* Also, Jeremiah 29:11 (KJV) says, *"For I know the thoughts that I think toward you, saith the LORD, thoughts of peace, and not of evil, to give you an expected end."*

The same was true for Moses. God had a specific plan for Moses. God's plan allowed Moses' life to be spared at his birth; God permitted Moses to be separated from his brethren and placed in Pharaoh's home while instilling in him a desire to connect with them; God allowed for Moses to escape Egypt and Pharaoh's wrath; God covered Moses from harm when he returned to Egypt to deliver God's message.

Let's continue to see exactly what God's plan was for Moses as it related to His chosen people.

One day as Moses was tending a flock of sheep, he came upon a burning bush near or at the base of Mount Sinai. Moses stared at the bush in wonderment, as he had never before encountered anything of that nature. Noticing that although the bush was aflame but it was not being consumed, Moses decided he would venture closer to look upon the spectacle.

When the Lord noticed Moses approaching closer to the bush, He saw He had been successful in gaining Moses' attention. Then, the Lord called to Moses from the interior of the bush. Hearing his name, Moses responded. Then, God told Moses to refrain from drawing nearer to the bush, for Moses had come close enough. Next, the Lord instructed Moses to remove his sandals stating the ground he was standing upon was holy ground. Desiring to be obedient and to honor the Lord, Moses immediately complied with God's instructions. Then, God introduced Himself to Moses saying, *"I am the God of your father – the God of Abraham, the God of Isaac, and the God of Jacob"* (Exodus 3:6, NLT).

When Moses heard the Lord's introduction, his hands suddenly covered his face because he feared looking upon God. As Moses stood in utter shock of the encounter he was experiencing, the Lord continued His monologue. He explained to Moses that He had witnessed the suffering of His people, the Israelites, at the hand of the Egyptians, and He had heard their cries of distress. He informed Moses that He would rescue them from the Egyptians and deliver them into the land flowing with milk and honey, the land that was currently inhabited by the Canaanites, Hittites, Amorites, Perizzites, Hivites, and Jebusites.

Even having said all of that, the Lord was not done. He had not simply visited Moses in such a dramatic way to tell him only that. No! The Lord was visiting Moses to give him a clarion call. All the preparation Moses had gone through for the last eighty years was for the assignment he was about to receive. The Lord told Moses, *"Now go, for I am sending you to Pharaoh. You must lead my people of Israel out of Egypt"* (Exodus 3:10, NLT).

Even though God's words were simple enough, to say Moses was astonished and bewildered by God's directive would be to state his disposition mildly. Moses' emotional and mental state can be easily discerned by the set of questions he posed to God. Moses asked, *"Who am I to appear before Pharaoh? Who am I to lead the people of Israel out of Egypt?"* (Exodus 3:11, NLT). Moses was clearly thrown for an unexpected curve when he heard the Lord's instructions. He had no idea how he could maneuver a feat of such great magnitude.

Detecting Moses' uncertainty and discomfort, God began to assure Moses that he would not be alone on his journey. However,

God's words did not soothe Moses' hesitancy. Moses continued to protest by asking who should he tell the Israelites had sent him if they should ask. Moses was not only concerned about the conversation he could potentially have with Pharaoh, but he was also concerned about having to answer to those he was going to save from bondage. God replied, *"Tell them I AM has sent me to you. Tell them Yahweh, the God of your ancestors – the God of Abraham, the God of Isaac, and the God of Jacob – has sent me to you"* (Exodus 3:14-15, NLT). Notice how God, knowing that moment was coming in Moses' life, had a ready answer for him.

Afterward, the Lord provided Moses more instructions that needed to be carried out prior to approaching Pharaoh and a few instructions that would be carried out throughout the process. For our purposes here, the verses that close Exodus Chapter 3 are of the utmost importance to lay the foundation of this book.

> *And I will cause the Egyptians to look favorably on you. They will give you gifts when you go so you will not leave empty-handed. Every Israelite woman will ask for articles of silver and gold and fine clothing from her Egyptian neighbors and from the foreign women in their houses. You would dress your sons and daughters with these, stripping the Egyptians of their wealth.*
> (Exodus 3:21-22)

In the final two verses of Chapter 3, the Lord foreshadowed the events that would take place upon the Israelites' exodus from Egypt. First, in verse 21, God proclaimed He would grant the Israelites favor with the Egyptians. The Egyptians' favor would be demonstrated in the way of gift giving to begin. Then, in verse 22, a directive for the Israelite women was given. On the eve of their exodus, the Israelite women were to ask of their Egyptian neighbors for articles of silver and gold and fine clothing.

When the Israelites departed from their land of slavery, they would not leave empty-handed. Instead, they would be equipped for their journey in the life that lay ahead and also when they arrived in the land of milk and honey: Canaan.

Now, let's move forward in time to gather more facts about the Exodus. Exodus Chapters 7-11 detail the plagues God sent upon Pharaoh and the Egyptians as a result of Pharaoh's continued refusal to release God's people, for God had hardened Pharaoh's heart. Plagues of blood, frogs, gnats, flies, livestock, festering boils, hail, locusts, and darkness fell upon the land. Throughout the duration of the plagues, God kept the Israelites safe. Then, the time finally came for the impending exodus, and God assured Moses that Pharaoh would release the Israelites once and for all. In preparation for the final plague – the death of Egypt's firstborn - the Lord gave Moses instructions for the Passover feast that the Israelites would eat on their final night in Egypt.

The Israelites, following the Lord's detailed instructions, prepared for the Passover feast and packed their personal belongings. That night, the Israelites observed the first Passover while being fully dressed, wearing their sandals, and carrying their walking sticks. At midnight, the final plague swept through Egypt. Although the other plagues were deadly, causing sickness and disease, none were like the final plague. The Death Plague of the Firstborn struck all the firstborn sons in the land of Egypt, from the firstborn son of Pharaoh to the firstborn son of the prisoner, including the firstborn of livestock, with exception to the Israelites who had obediently placed blood on their doorposts from specifically chosen one-year-old lambs that bore no spot or blemish. Upon witnessing the deaths, loud wailing was heard throughout the land.

After the bloodshed, Pharaoh sent for Moses and his brother Aaron and ordered them, along with the rest of the Israelites, out of Egypt. Finally, God's command had manifested. There was just one thing left for the Israelites to do. God had set a provision in place, and all the Israelites had to do was tap into it by trusting God's word that had been delivered by Moses.

In Chapter 12, verses 35-36 (NLT), we read, *"... [T]he people of Israel did as Moses had instructed; they asked the Egyptians for clothing and articles of silver and gold. The Lord caused the Egyptians to look favorably on the Israelites, and they gave the Israelites whatever they asked for. So, they stripped the Egyptians of their wealth!"* And, with the gold and silver, the Israelites departed Egypt beginning their exodus to the Promised Land, as they looked forward to a new life with God's power and protection over-shadowing them.

The Israelites, who had been mistreated for over 400 years, who had been enslaved, who had their rights and privileges stripped away generation after generation while living in an estranged land, had the privilege of the one true living God, Yahweh, come to their rescue, saying, *"I have certainly seen the oppression of my people... I have heard their cries of distress... I am aware of their suffering"* (Exodus 3:7, NLT).

The Israelites had cried out for many years to God for His assistance. Finally, in due season, God answered the Israelites' prayers, setting them free from a detestable life of bondage, pain, and suffering.

The Israelites are not the only group of people that have been held in bondage. In many places throughout the world, the same condition has been found in nearly every time period. Bondage does not only manifest in the form of physical restraint. Rather, it is demonstrated in variable structures from racism, discri-mination, prejudice, social status, economic status, educational limitations, lack of adequate healthcare provisions, lack of proper housing, inequities, inequalities, and the list goes on.

Regardless of the type of bondage a person is entrapped in, what is important to note is what Apostle Peter proclaims in Acts 10:34 (ESV): *"Truly I understand that God shows no partiality."* That means although partiality is overwrought and rampant in the world system, God, our creator, does not show favoritism. So, when deciding whom He will rescue in the time of need, His love and care will be demonstrated to all His people. Therefore, regardless of what ensnares a person, God is able and willing to free the person from unfair treatment suffered unduly at the hands of other people.

Not only is God not a respecter of persons, but in Ephesians 1:5, Apostle Paul wrote, *"God decided in advance to adopt us into his own family by bringing us to himself through Jesus Christ. This is what he wanted to do, and it gave him great pleasure."* Because we have been adopted into the family of God, we too have access to the throne of God where we can make our petitions known unto Him, *AND* we have Jesus, sitting on God's right hand, making intercession for us.

Finally, to further demonstrate God's love and desire to rescue those in need, I provide you Matthew 7:11 (NLT), *"So if you sinful people know how to give good gifts to your children, how much more will your heavenly Father give good gifts to those who ask him."* If sinful people seek to hurt us and try to cover it up by periodically providing us with what appears only on the surface to be a good gift, when in actuality it is only a salve over a wound, we can expect for God to render unto us what is truly good and in our best interest if we ask Him.

So, the key to being delivered from an unwanted and troubling situation is to ask God for a timely reprieve of the situation. Ask! Then, let God do the rest. He will certainly hear your cry, as He heard the Israelites' cries, and in due season, if you faint not, He will rescue you!

Chapter Two

God Has the Final Word

"So those who are last now will be first then,
and those who are first will be last."
Matthew 20:16 (NLT)

The above verse is the final statement Jesus made after He shared the Parable of the Vineyard Workers. Here is the parable in its entirety from Matthew 20:1-16:

> For the Kingdom of Heaven is like the landowner who went out early one morning to hire workers for his vineyard. ² He agreed to pay the normal daily wage[a] and sent them out to work. ³ "At nine o'clock in the morning he was passing through the marketplace and saw some people standing around doing nothing. ⁴ So he hired them, telling them he would pay them whatever was right at the end of the day. ⁵ So they went to work in the vineyard. At noon and again at three o'clock he did the same thing. ⁶ "At five o'clock that afternoon he was in town again and saw some more people standing around. He asked them, 'Why haven't you

been working today?' 7 "They replied, 'Because no one hired us.' "The landowner told them, 'Then go out and join the others in my vineyard.' 8 "That evening he told the foreman to call the workers in and pay them, beginning with the last workers first. 9 When those hired at five o'clock were paid, each received a full day's wage. 10 When those hired first came to get their pay, they assumed they would receive more. But they, too, were paid a day's wage. 11 When they received their pay, they protested to the owner, 12 'Those people worked only one hour, and yet you've paid them just as much as you paid us who worked all day in the scorching heat.' 13 "He answered one of them, 'Friend, I haven't been unfair! Didn't you agree to work all day for the usual wage? 14 Take your money and go. I wanted to pay this last worker the same as you. 15 Is it against the law for me to do what I want with my money? Should you be jealous because I am kind to others?' 16 "So those who are last now will be first then, and those who are first will be last.

Just as it was with the workers in the Lord's parable, it seems to be human nature to oftentimes bring up what is fair or not fair solely based on one's perspective or calculated assessment of a given situation. Individuals tend to present to others their limited worldview, which is based on their belief of what is equal treatment and which, of course, is completely subjective. This type of dialogue quite often can be witnessed amongst adolescents whose version of the world revolves around life being fair. Here's an example: A parent gives two children a slice of pie each, but one slice is bigger than the other. The child with the smallest slice is likely to complain even if he or she does not particularly care for the type of pie. For the disgruntled child, it does not factor in whether he or she dislikes the pie, he or she just desires and expects equal and fair treatment from the parent. Anything less than the same size piece of pie is viewed as unfair treatment.

This reminds me of an occasion when my two-year-old grandson was over for a visit. On that night, I prepared hard-shell tacos for dinner. Knowing that young kids do not typically desire to eat hard-shell tacos, I decided to give him the fillings of the taco in a bowl with no shell. After placing his bowl of taco meat and cheese in front of him, I commenced preparing tacos for myself and placed them on a plate. I told my grandson to say his grace and to begin eating his food. His eyes quickly darted from my plate to his and back again. Before beginning to eat or saying his grace, he asked me, "I'm eating this?" with a scowl upon his face and a pointed finger aimed at his bowl. I looked at him and calmly answered, "Yes," wondering what his issue was.

For what appeared to be several minutes, my grandson looked at me without saying anything. I was seriously being challenged by a two-year-old on his eating preferences. I had to convince him that the ground taco meat was delicious before he would pick up his spoon and begin to eat. After he ate a few bites, he kept staring at my tacos in silent protest. He obviously was not convinced that his food was equivalent to mine. Not wanting to be stared down, I asked him if he wanted a taco shell, to which he answered affirmatively. I chastised him about not wasting taco shells and that he had better eat it. He assured me he would, so I prepared him a taco that was somewhat similar to mine (minus the lettuce, tomatoes, and onions). When I handed the taco over to him, he promptly began to eat it and was happy to do so. Notice this - my grandson felt his dinner was inferior to mine. Although he was half a century younger than I was, he wanted to be treated fairly and eat what I was eating. And, as you can see- I relented.

Not only is fair and equal treatment sought in everyday life by citizens of all ages, races, cultures, and nationalities as they engage with one another, whether during ancient times as in the parable or present day, but also when it comes to legal matters. Our courts strive to enforce guidelines regarding equality that are embedded within the United States Constitution, which was written in 1787, but specifically in accordance with the Fourteenth Amendment's Equal Protection Clause (EPC), ratified in 1868. The EPC states, "No State shall make or enforce any law which shall abridge the privileges or immunities of citizens of the United States; nor shall any State deprive any person of life, liberty, or property, without due process of law; nor deny to any person within its jurisdiction the equal protection of the laws."

From the States' acceptance of the original constitution to the ratification of the Fourteen Amendment, eighty-one years had passed before country leaders saw the proverbial light. But to give the United States some credit, changes were being made to benefit all citizens, even if those changes are still moving at horse and buggy pace (to quote Dr. Martin Luther King, Jr.).

But, let's take a step back and delve a little deeper into our discussion of fair and equal treatment as it is viewed in terms of our United States laws. Prior to the ratification and enforcement of the Fourteenth Amendment was the ratification of the Thirteenth Amendment in 1864, which states in Section 1: "Neither slavery nor involuntary servitude, except as a punishment for crime whereof the party shall have been duly convicted, shall exist within the United States, or any place subject to their jurisdiction."

Notice how the Fourteenth Amendment's EPC clause along with Section 1 of the Thirteenth Amendment changed governmental outlook toward all persons from an original statement in Article 1, Section 2, Clause 2 of the United States Constitution, which states, "Representatives and direct Taxes shall be apportioned among the several States which may be included within this Union, according to their respective Numbers, which shall be determined by adding to the whole Number of free Persons, including those bound to Service for a Term of Years, and excluding Indians not taxed, three fifths of all other Persons." This statement demonstrates the legality of slavery prior to and at the time of the Constitution's composition. However, in an effort to hold to the statutes outlined in the Emancipation Proclamation of 1862, that article was amended with use of the Thirteenth Amendment.

Moreover, the preamble of the Declaration of Independence, penned in 1776, states, "We hold these truths to be self-evident, that all men are created equal, that they are endowed by their Creator with certain unalienable Rights, that among these are Life, Liberty and the pursuit of Happiness." This document provides further evidence that it has always been a human desire (from most but not all individuals) that all persons be treated fairly.

The Declaration of Independence was written in 1776 while the United States Constitution was written in 1787. Looking at the dates the two documents were written and noticing the incongruency between the two, you may be wondering, "How can one document discuss equality and unalienable rights while the other discusses slavery and the value of a man being equated to three-fifths of a person?" This is the short answer: The United States Constitution is a legal document and therefore enforceable, while the Declaration of Independence is not.

Therefore, the powerfully stated words that comprise the Declaration of Independence are just that- words on a page, with no legal authority to present the existence of laws ratified in a court. Conclusively, the strong and powerful words stated in the nationally acclaimed document from the desk of one of the nation's founding fathers (Thomas Jefferson) could easily lead one to believe that the very country in which the document was dispersed would certainly be a country that practices what it "preaches" – using the word loosely, of course.

Conversely, in this same country in which both of the aforementioned documents (the United States Constitution with all of its amendments and the Emancipation Proclamation) were composed, one would believe equal treatment of its citizens, which is hereby protected under law, would be dispensed across the board. But anyone who resides in this country and watches, listens to, or reads the news knows that statement is a FALLACY. Each and every day, without fail, injustices are rampant and pervasive throughout the United States.

Dr. King said it well in "Letter from Birmingham Jail," (1963) which eventually became a chapter of his novel titled *Why We Can't Wait*: "...when you are forever fighting a degenerating sense of 'nobodiness' - then you will understand why we find it difficult to wait. There comes a time when the cup of endurance runs over, and men are no longer willing to be plunged into the abyss of despair." People want and deserve equal and fair treatment, and they should not have to wait for it.

Interestingly, Dr. King's statement was written in the early 1960's. However, prior to that timeframe, the sentiments of Blacks were the same. In present day, the sentiments have yet to dissipate. To shed a bit more light on this ever-looming issue, President Barack Obama quoted a passage from of W.E.B. Du Bois' *The Souls of Black Folk*, which was published in 1903, in his own novel *A Promised Land* (2020). Obama's citing of Du Bois indicates the prejudices which were rampant throughout the 1900s are still prevalent today. Obama wrote:

> In THE SOULS OF BLACK FOLK, the sociologist W.E.B. Du Bois describes the "double consciousness" of Black Americans at the dawn of the twentieth century. Despite having been born and raised on American soil, shaped by this nation's institutions and infused with its creed, despite the fact that their toiling hands and beating hearts contributed so much to the country's economy and culture

- despite all this, Du Bois writes, Black Americans remain the perpetual "Other," always on the outside looking in, ever feeling their "two-ness," defined not by what they are but what they can never be. (p. 131)

To be fair, Obama does mention that growing up, he never experienced the 'double consciousness' that Du Bois wrote about or questioned his "Americanness." Well... not until he ran for the presidency. There is always a point in a person of color's life when he/she will feel the double consciousness.

To demonstrate the rampant existence of inequalities and inequities that exist in times past and present day, let us take a moment to survey a few examples of injustices that have occurred throughout history.

Emmett Till – lynched in 1955

On August 24, while standing with his cousins and some friends outside a country store in Money, Mississippi, Emmett Till, a 14-year-old African-American, who was visiting from the southside of Chicago, bragged that his girlfriend back home was white. Emmett's African American companions, disbelieving him, dared Emmett to ask the white woman sitting behind the store counter for a date.

He went in, bought some candy, and on the way out was heard saying, "Bye, baby" to the woman. There were no witnesses in the store, but Carolyn Bryant, the woman behind the counter, later claimed that he grabbed her, made lewd advances and wolf-whistled at her as he sauntered out.

Roy Bryant, the proprietor of the store and the woman's husband, returned from a business trip a few days later and heard how Emmett had allegedly spoken to his wife. Enraged, he went to the home of Till's great uncle, Mose Wright, with his half-brother J.W. Milam in the early morning hours of August 28.

The pair demanded to see the boy. Despite pleas from Wright, they forced Emmett into their car. After driving around in the night, and perhaps beating Till in a tool house behind Milam's residence, they drove him down to the Tallahatchie River.

His assailants -the white woman's husband and her brother-made Emmett carry a 75-pound cotton-gin fan to the bank of the Tallahatchie River and ordered him to take off his clothes. The two men then beat him nearly to death, gouged out his eye, shot him in the head and then threw his body, tied to the cotton-gin fan with barbed wire, into the river.

Three days later, his corpse was recovered but was so disfigured that Mose Wright could only identify it by an initialed ring. Authorities wanted to bury the body quickly, but Till's mother, Mamie Bradley, requested it be sent back to Chicago.

After seeing the mutilated remains, she decided to have an open-casket funeral so that all the world could see what racist murderers had done to her only son. Jet, an African American weekly magazine, published a photo of Emmett's corpse, and soon the mainstream media picked up on the story.

Less than two weeks after Emmett's body was buried, Milam and Bryant went on trial in a segregated courthouse in Sumner, Mississippi. There were few witnesses besides Mose Wright, who positively identified the defendants as Emmett's killers.

On September 23, the all-white jury deliberated for less than an hour before issuing a verdict of "not guilty," explaining that they believed the state had failed to prove the identity of the body. Many people around the country were outraged by the decision and also by the state's decision not to indict Milam and Bryant on the separate charge of kidnapping.

The Emmett Till murder trial brought to light the brutality of Jim Crow segregation in the South and was an early impetus of the Civil Rights Movement.

In 2017, Tim Tyson, author of the book *The Blood of Emmett Till*, revealed that Carolyn Bryant recanted her testimony, admitting that Till had never touched, threatened or harassed her. "Nothing that boy did could ever justify what happened to him," she said.
("Emmet Till is Murdered." history.com. August 28, 1955. Reviewed on November 30, 2020.)

Medgar Evans - killed in 1963

Medgar Evers was a native of Decatur, Mississippi, attending school there until being inducted into the U.S. Army in 1943. Despite fighting for his country as part of the Battle of Normandy, Evers soon found that his skin color gave him no freedom when he and five friends were forced away at gunpoint from voting in a local election. Despite his resentment over such treatment, Evers enrolled at Alcorn State University, majoring in business administration.

Evers applied to the then-segregated University of Mississippi Law School in February 1954. When his application was rejected, Evers became the focus of an NAACP campaign to desegregate the school, a case aided by the U.S. Supreme Court ruling in the case of Brown v. Board of Education 347 US 483 that segregation was unconstitutional. In December of that year, Evers became the NAACP's first field officer in Mississippi.

After moving to Jackson, he was involved in a boycott campaign against white merchants and was instrumental in eventually desegregating the University of Mississippi when that institution was finally forced to enroll James Meredith in 1962.

In the weeks leading up to his death, Evers found himself the target of a number of threats. His public investigations into the murder of Emmett Till and his vocal support of Clyde Kennard left him vulnerable to attack. On May 28, 1963, a molotov cocktail was thrown into the carport of his home, and five days before his death, he was nearly run down by a car after he emerged from the Jackson NAACP office. Civil rights demonstrations accelerated in Jackson during the first week of June 1963. A local television station granted Evers time for a short speech, his first in Mississippi, where he outlined the goals of the Jackson movement. Following the speech, threats on Evers' life increased.

On June 12, 1963, Evers pulled into his driveway after returning from an integration meeting where he had conferred with NAACP lawyers. Emerging from his car and carrying NAACP T-shirts that stated, "Jim Crow Must Go", Evers was struck in the back with a bullet that ricocheted into his home. He staggered 30 feet before collapsing, dying at the local hospital 50 minutes later. Evers was murdered just hours after President John F. Kennedy's speech on national television in support of civil rights.

Mourned nationally, Evers was buried on June 19 in Arlington National Cemetery and received full military honors in front of a crowd of more than 3,000 people, the largest funeral at Arlington since John Foster Dulles. The past chairman of the American Veterans Committee, Mickey Levine, said at the services, "No soldier in this field has fought more courageously, more heroically than Medgar Evers."

On June 23, Byron De La Beckwith, a fertilizer salesman and member of the White Citizens' Council and Ku Klux Klan, was arrested for Evers' murder. During the course of his first 1964 trial, De La Beckwith was visited by former Mississippi governor Ross Barnett and one-time Army Major General Edwin A. Walker.

All-white juries twice that year deadlocked on De La Beckwith's guilt, allowing him to escape justice.

("NAACP History: Medgar Evers." naacp.com. 2020. Reviewed on November 30, 2020.)

Rodney King - beaten by the police in 1991

On March 3, 1991, King was beaten by LAPD officers after a high-speed chase during his arrest for drunk driving on I-210. A civilian, George Holliday, filmed the incident from his nearby balcony and sent the footage to local news station KTLA. The footage showed an unarmed King on the ground being beaten after initially evading arrest. The incident was covered by news media around the world and caused a public furor.

At a press conference, announcing the four officers involved would be disciplined, and three would face criminal charges, Los Angeles police chief Daryl Gates said: "We believe the officers used excessive force taking him into custody. In our review, we find that officers struck him with batons between fifty-three and fifty-six times." The LAPD initially charged King with "felony evading," but later dropped the charge. On his release, he spoke to reporters from his wheelchair, with his injuries evident: a broken right leg in a cast, his face badly cut and swollen, bruises on his body, and a burn area to his chest where he had been jolted with a 50,000-volt stun gun. He described how he had knelt, spread his hands out, and slowly tried to move so as not to make any 'stupid move,' being hit across the face by a billy club and shocked. He said he was scared for his life as they drew down on him.

Four officers were eventually tried on charges of use of excessive force. Of these, three were acquitted, and the jury failed to reach a verdict on one charge for the fourth. Within hours of the acquittals, the 1992 Los Angeles riots started, sparked by outrage among racial minorities over the trial's verdict and related, longstanding social issues. The rioting lasted six days and killed 63 people, with 2,383 more injured; it ended only after the California Army National Guard, the United States Army, and the United States Marine Corps provided reinforcements to re-establish control. The federal government prosecuted a separate civil rights case, obtaining grand jury indictments of the four officers for violations of King's civil rights. Their trial in a federal district court ended on April 16, 1993, with two of the officers being found guilty and sentenced to serve prison terms. The other two were acquitted of the charges. In a separate civil lawsuit in 1994, a jury found the city of Los Angeles liable and awarded King $3.8 million in damages.

(Pulled from a variety of sources. Reviewed on November 30, 2020.)

Trayvon Martin - shot and killed in 2012

Trayvon Martin, a 17-year-old African American, was returning from a convenience store when he was noticed by Zimmerman, a neighborhood-watch volunteer of German and Peruvian ancestry. Zimmerman contacted the nonemergency line of the Sanford Police Department, mentioned that there had been burglaries in the neighborhood, and told the dispatcher that he had observed "a real suspicious guy" who was "walking around, looking about." Zimmerman also described Martin as someone "up to no good, or he's on drugs or something." The dispatcher communicated to Zimmerman that the police did not need him to follow Martin, but Zimmerman, nevertheless, left his vehicle. He later said he had done so in order to ascertain his location by taking a closer look at a street sign. A violent confrontation ensued, and Zimmerman fired his weapon at Martin at close range, causing Martin's death. When police arrived, Zimmerman argued that he had been assaulted by Martin, who was unarmed, and fired in self-defense. Concluding that they could not hold Zimmerman - because no evidence contradicted his version of the event and because state law permitted the use of deadly force in self-defense - the police released him.

In the following weeks, as Zimmerman remained uncharged, the shooting drew increasing attention. On March 12, the chief of the Sanford Police Department affirmed that no criminal charge could be filed against Zimmerman, mainly because of the absence of probable cause. A day later, however, a Sanford police investigator assigned to the case recommended that Zimmerman be charged with manslaughter, on the basis that the violent encounter between the two men could have been avoided. Zimmerman remained free, which was seen by many as an injustice, and demonstrations demanding his prosecution for murder were organized in cities across the United States. In April 2012 the governor of Florida, Rick Scott, appointed a special prosecutor for the case, who brought a criminal charge of second-degree murder against Zimmerman.

Zimmerman's trial - which began more than a year later, in June 2013 - received intensive media coverage. The prosecution argued that Martin's death resulted from Zimmerman's profiling of him as a criminal and trying to take the law into his own hands. The defense argued that the evidence corroborated Zimmerman's version of the event -namely, that he fired his weapon because Martin was attacking him and that he felt that his life was threatened. Central elements of the incident, however, could not be ascertained. For instance, witnesses disagreed on which of the two men could be heard screaming for help on a recorded call to emergency services.

Although the original criminal charge brought against Zimmerman was second-degree murder, the judge also gave the jury the option of convicting him of the lesser charge of manslaughter. In order to find Zimmerman guilty of second-degree murder or manslaughter, the jury had to find not only that Zimmerman had caused Martin's death but also that he did not do so in self-defense. The issue of self-defense was linked to Florida's law permitting the use of deadly force to defend oneself against a perceived threat - known as a "stand-your-ground" law - which was central to debate over the shooting. Instructions to the jury referenced the law, but Zimmerman's lawyers ultimately did not invoke Zimmerman's rights under it, because, they argued, he did not have the option to retreat anyway. On July 13, 2013, after more than 16 hours of deliberation, the jury declared Zimmerman not guilty.

Martin's death heightened a debate over the persistence of racism in the United States and in particular over the issue of racial profiling. In March 2012 Pres. Barack Obama - the first African American president of the United States - expressed his dismay at the shooting, saying that "if I had a son, he'd look like Trayvon." Later Obama compared Martin to his younger self and characterized racial profiling as a reality that most African Americans, including himself, have had to face. Protests continued across the United States in the wake of the Zimmerman verdict and led to the formation of the prominent Black Lives Matter social movement, which focused on better treatment of African Americans in all facets of American society.
(Munro, Andre. "The Shooting of Trayvon Martin." June 29, 2015. Reviewed on November 30, 2020.)

Four Congresswomen - belittled by President Trump in 2019

Going after four Democratic congresswomen one by one, a combative President Donald Trump turned his campaign rally into an extended dissection of the liberal views of the women of color, deriding them for what he painted as extreme positions and suggesting they just get out.

"Tonight I have a suggestion for the hate-filled extremists who are constantly trying to tear our country down," Trump told the crowd in North Carolina, a swing state he won in 2016 and wants to claim again in 2020. "They never have anything good to say. That's why I say, 'Hey if you don't like it, let 'em leave, let 'em leave.'"

Eager to rile up his base with the some of the same kind of rhetoric he targeted at minorities and women in 2016, Trump declared Wednesday night, "I think in some cases they hate our country."

Trump's jabs were aimed at the self-described "squad" of four freshmen Democrats who have garnered attention since their arrival in January for their outspoken liberal views and distaste for Trump: Reps. Alexandria Ocasio-Cortez of New York, Ilhan Omar of Minnesota, Ayanna Pressley of Massachusetts and Rashida Tlaib of Michigan. All were born in the U.S. except for Omar, who came to the U.S. as a child after fleeing Somalia with her family.

(Riechmann, Deb. "Trump blasts 4 congresswomen; crowd roars, 'Send her back!'" July 18, 2019. Reviewed on November 30, 2020.)

Breonna Taylor - shot by a police officer in 2020

According to the Taylor family's lawsuit, plainclothes police officers arrived at Taylor's apartment at around 12:30 a.m. on March 13. Taylor and her boyfriend, Kenneth Walker, were asleep in a bedroom and woke up suddenly, believing that someone was breaking in. Police officers - later identified as Jonathan Mattingly, Brett Hankison, and Myles Cosgrove - entered "without knocking and without announcing themselves as police officers," the lawsuit says. LMPD insists they "knocked on the door several times and announced their presence as police who were there with a search warrant." The lawsuit contends that multiple neighbors gave statements contradicting this claim.

On May 22, 2020, county prosecutor Tom Wine held a press conference in which he played audio from Walker's police interrogation. Walker said that "there was a loud bang at the door," but no one said they were police. Walker said Taylor asked multiple times "at the top of her lungs," "Who is it?" "Nobody announced themselves or anything," Walker says in the audio. "If I would have heard at the door, 'It's the police,' it changes the whole situation. There's nothing for us to be scared of ... We could have opened the door like, 'What's the problem, what's going on?' ... The only reason I had the gun was because we didn't know who it was, if we knew who it was that would have never happened."

"While police may claim to have identified themselves, they did not. Mr. Walker and Ms. Taylor again heard a large bang on the door," Walker's attorney wrote in a motion. "Again, when they inquired there was no response that there [were] police outside. At this point, the door suddenly explodes. Counsel believes that police hit the door with a battering ram." In the interrogation audio, Walker said the door "came off its hinges."

Taylor's mother told the Washington *Post* that she had received a call from Walker, who said someone was trying to break into the apartment before shouting, "I think they shot Breonna." According to his attorney, Walker fired a shot in self-defense and struck an officer in the leg. Walker is a licensed firearm carrier. In response, police opened fire, shooting more than 20 rounds into Taylor's home, striking objects in the living room, dining room, kitchen, hallway, bathroom, and both bedrooms. Taylor was shot at least eight times and was pronounced dead at the scene.

Walker was arrested and charged with assault and attempted murder on a police officer. Later in the month, he was released from jail on home incarceration, and on May 26, the charges against him were dismissed. The three officers involved in the shooting were placed on administrative reassignment pending the outcome of an investigation in May.
(Read, Bridget. "What We Know About the Killing of Breonna Taylor." September 29, 2020. November 30, 2020.)

A grand jury indicted a former Louisville police officer in late September for wanton endangerment for his actions during the raid. He pleaded not guilty. No charges were announced against the other two officers who fired shots, and no one was charged for causing Ms. Taylor's death.

After months of protests that turned Breonna Taylor's name into a national slogan against police violence, city officials agreed to pay her family $12 million and institute changes aimed at preventing future deaths by officers.
(Callimachi, Rukmini. "Breonna Taylor's Family to Receive $12 Million Settlement From City of Louisville." Nytimes.com. September 15, 2020. Reviewed on November 30, 2020.)

With this next case that received national attention, we can see changes being made within our justice system with quicker actions in regards to treatment and charges filed against the accused. However, who is to say that the reaction wasn't just a response to the media attention the case was getting. Who knows if the response would have been the same in a lesser known case?

George Floyd – executed by police in 2020
On May 25, Minneapolis police officers arrested George Floyd, a 46-year-old black man, after a convenience store employee called 911 and told the police that Mr. Floyd had bought cigarettes with a counterfeit $20 bill. Seventeen minutes after the first squad car arrived at the scene, Mr. Floyd was unconscious and pinned beneath three police officers, showing no signs of life.

By combining videos from bystanders and security cameras, reviewing official documents and consulting experts, The New York Times reconstructed in detail the minutes leading to Mr. Floyd's death. Our video shows officers taking a series of actions that violated the policies of the Minneapolis Police Department and turned fatal, leaving Mr. Floyd unable to breathe, even as he and onlookers called out for help.

The day after Mr. Floyd's death, the Police Department fired all four of the officers involved in the episode. On May 29, the Hennepin County attorney, Mike Freeman, announced third-degree murder and second-degree manslaughter charges against Derek Chauvin, the officer seen most clearly in witness videos pinning Mr. Floyd to the ground. Mr. Chauvin, who is white, kept his knee on Mr. Floyd's neck for at least eight minutes and 15 seconds, according to a Times analysis of timestamped video. Our video investigation shows that Mr. Chauvin did not remove his knee even after Mr. Floyd lost consciousness and for a full minute and 20 seconds after paramedics arrived at the scene.

On June 3, Hennepin County prosecutors added a more serious second-degree murder charge against Mr. Chauvin and also charged each of the three other former officers - Thomas Lane, J. Alexander Kueng and Tou Thao - with aiding and abetting second-degree murder.

On June 18, the Hennepin County attorney's office said that its criminal complaint misstated the amount of time Mr. Chauvin kept his knee on Mr. Floyd's neck. The complaint originally said that Mr. Chauvin had done so for eight minutes and 46 seconds, a length of time that became a symbol and rallying cry for protesters. Responding to inquiries from journalists who noted a discrepancy with the durations listed in the complaint, the office said the actual time was seven minutes and 46 seconds. But The Times' own analysis of the video shows that this revised time is also incorrect.

"It makes no difference," said Jamar Nelson, who works with the families of crime victims in Minneapolis. "The bottom line is, it was long enough to kill him, long enough to execute him."
(Hill, Evan. "How George Floyd was Killed in Police Custody. nytimes.com. May 31, 2020. Reviewed on November 30, 2020.)

In addition to the cases discussed and many others that may not be as widely known, discussed or documented, unequal treatment can also be seen in cases were officers were exonerated after "allegedly" committing illegal acts. Read the following document from *Police Integrity Research Group* from Bowling Group State University released in 2019.

On-Duty Shootings: Police Officers Charged with Murder or Manslaughter, 2005-2019
Philip M. Stinson, Sr. & Chloe A. Wentzlof

Background- This research is part of a larger study of police crime - that is, crime committed by nonfederal sworn law enforcement officers with general powers of arrest - across the United States. In 2014, after several fatal on-duty police shootings garnered national media attention, our principal investigator, Philip Stinson, conducted a joint research project with The Washington Post to count the number of police officers charged with murder or manslaughter resulting from an on-duty shooting where the officer shot and killed someone. The results of the joint research project were published in The Washington Post on April 12, 2015, and The Washington Post was awarded the 2016 Pulitzer Prize for National Reporting, in part, for this project. The Police Integrity Research Group at Bowling Green State University continues to keep the information current, and new cases are added periodically to the count of officers charged with murder or manslaughter resulting from an on-duty shooting.

Findings- Since the beginning of 2005 (through June 24, 2019), there have been 104 nonfederal sworn law enforcement officers with the general powers of arrest (e.g., police officers, deputy sheriffs, state troopers, etc.) who have been arrested for murder or manslaughter resulting from an on-duty shooting where the officer shot and killed someone at incidents throughout the United States. Of those 104 officers, to date only 35 have been convicted of a crime resulting from the on-duty shooting (15 by guilty plea, 20 by jury trial, and none convicted by a bench trial). In the cases where an officer has been convicted, it is often for a lesser offense. Only 4 officers have been convicted of murder (there were four officers whose murder convictions were overturned, but the officers were later convicted of federal crimes arising out of the same incident).

In the cases where an officer has been convicted, it is often for a lesser offense. Only 4 officers have been convicted of murder (there were four officers whose murder convictions were overturned, but the officers were later convicted of federal crimes arising out of the same incident). The 4 officers convicted of murder received incarceration sentences that ranged from 81 months to 192 months in prison, with an average length prison sentence of 150.75 months.

As to the other officers, 9 were convicted of manslaughter, 4 were convicted of voluntary manslaughter, 5 were convicted of involuntary manslaughter, 2 were convicted of official misconduct, 2 were convicted of reckless homicide, 3 were convicted of negligent homicide, 5 were convicted of federal criminal deprivation of civil rights (including the four officers whose murder convictions were overturned), and one was convicted of reckless discharge of a firearm. The 18 officers convicted of manslaughter received incarceration sentences that ranged from zero months to 480 months in prison, with an average sentence of 78.5 months in prison.

The criminal cases for 45 of the officers ended in a non-conviction: 23 were acquitted at a jury trial, 9 were acquitted at a bench trial, 4 were dismissed by a judge, 7 were dismissed by a prosecutor, one received a deferred adjudication, and in one instance no true bill was returned from a grand jury.

Out of the 104 officers charged since the beginning of 2005 with murder or manslaughter resulting from an on-duty shooting, the criminal cases have been concluded for 80 of the officers (35 convicted and 45 not convicted). The criminal cases for 24 of the officers are still pending today.

RACE DATA FOR COMPLETED CASES:

Non-Black Officers: 29 convicted (victims in these cases: 19 Black, 10 Non-Black) 38 not convicted (victims in these cases: 21 Black, 17 Non-Black) Black Officers: 6 convicted (victims in these cases: 3 Black, 3 Non-Black) 7 not convicted (All 7 victims were also Black) Note that there have been 35 officers convicted in one of these cases. The victims in 22 of those 35 cases were Black.

VICTIMS WITH DANGEROUS WEAPONS:

When looking at the cases of the 104 officers who were charged with murder or manslaughter resulting from an on-duty shooting, 33 (31.7%) involved a victim who was actually armed with a dangerous weapon (e.g., gun, bat, scissors, screwdriver, automobile) when they were shot and killed by the police. To date, only 35 officers have been convicted of a crime, and just 10 (28.6%) of those cases involved a victim who was actually armed with a dangerous weapon when they were shot and killed by the police. When looking at the 45 cases that ended in a nonconviction for the officer, 14 (31.1%) of those cases involved a victim who was actually armed with a dangerous weapon when they were shot and killed by the police. When looking at the 24 cases still pending in court, 9 (37.5%) of those cases involve a victim who was actually armed with a dangerous weapon when they were shot and killed by the police.

VICTIMS WITH GUNS:

When looking at the cases of the 104 officers who were charged with murder of manslaughter resulting from an on-duty shooting, 12 (11.5%) involved a victim who was actually armed with a gun when they were shot and killed by the police. To date, only 35 officers have been convicted of a crime, and just 3 (8.6%) of those cases involved a victim who was actually armed with a gun when they were shot and killed by the police. When looking at the 45 cases that ended in a nonconviction for the officer, 5 (11.1%) of those cases involved a victim who was actually armed with a gun when they were shot and killed by the police. When looking at the 24 cases still pending in court, 4 (16.7%) of those cases involve a victim who was actually armed with a gun when they were shot and killed by the police.

With all the provided examples of citizens crying out for justice to be served in their individual cases, it is easily discerned that the United States Constitution is not being upheld equally for all citizens. And while I would recommend each person who believes him/herself to have been underserved by our judicial system to seek justice and to cry out loud, I see a much more powerful and effective avenue that can be taken.

From the overview provided in the first chapter of this book, we saw a mighty move of God manifested in the life of the Israelites. God Himself said He heard their cries of distress. Do you think He will not hear your cry? Do you think God's ears are too dim to hear and that His arms are too short to reach out to you?

The faith of the Israelites in the God of their forefathers, the God of Abraham, the God of Isaac, and the God of Jacob, prevailed in their life. How strong is your faith? Do you have enough faith to move the mountain that is in your life?

Let's read Hebrews Chapter 11 in its entirety to be reminded of the power of faith.

> Now faith is the substance of things hoped for, the evidence of things not seen. ² For by it the elders obtained a good testimony. ³ By faith we understand that the worlds were framed by the word of God, so that the things which are seen were not made of things which are visible. ⁴ By faith Abel offered to God a more excellent sacrifice than Cain, through which he obtained witness that he was righteous, God testifying of his gifts; and through it he being dead still speaks ⁵ By faith Enoch was taken away so that he did not see death, "and was not found, because God had taken him"; for before he was taken he had this testimony, that he pleased God. ⁶ But without faith it is impossible to please Him, for he who comes to God must believe that He is, and that He is a rewarder of those who diligently seek Him.

7 By faith Noah, being divinely warned of things not yet seen, moved with godly fear, prepared an ark for the saving of his household, by which he condemned the world and became heir of the righteousness which is according to faith. 8 By faith Abraham obeyed when he was called to go out to the place which he would receive as an inheritance. And he went out, not knowing where he was going. 9 By faith he dwelt in the land of promise as in a foreign country, dwelling in tents with Isaac and Jacob, the heirs with him of the same promise; 10 for he waited for the city which has foundations, whose builder and maker is God. 11 By faith Sarah herself also received strength to conceive seed, and she bore a child when she was past the age, because she judged Him faithful who had promised. 12 Therefore from one man, and him as good as dead, were born as many as the stars of the sky in multitude—innumerable as the sand which is by the seashore. 13 These all died in faith, not having received the promises, but having seen them afar off [e] were assured of them, embraced them and confessed that they were strangers and pilgrims on the earth. 14 For those who say such things declare plainly that they seek a homeland. 15 And truly if they had called to mind that country from which they had come out, they would have had opportunity to return. 16 But now they desire a better, that is, a heavenly country. Therefore God is not ashamed to be called their God, for He has prepared a city for them. 17 By faith Abraham, when he was tested, offered up Isaac, and he who had received the promises offered up his only begotten son, 18 of whom it was said, "In Isaac your seed shall be called," 19 concluding that God was able to raise him up, even from the dead, from which he also received him in a figurative sense. 20 By faith Isaac blessed Jacob and Esau concerning things to come. 21 By faith Jacob, when he was dying, blessed each of the sons of Joseph, and worshiped, leaning on the top of his staff. ²² By faith Joseph, when he was dying, made mention of the departure of the children of Israel, and gave instructions concerning his bones. ²³ By faith Moses, when he was born, was hidden three months by his parents, because they saw he was a beautiful child; and they were not afraid of the king's command. ²⁴ By faith Moses, when he became of age, refused to be called the son of Pharaoh's daughter, ²⁵ choosing rather to suffer affliction with the people of God than to enjoy the passing pleasures of sin, ²⁶ esteeming the reproach of Christ greater riches than the treasures in Egypt; for he looked to the reward. ²⁷ By faith he forsook Egypt, not fearing the wrath of the king; for he endured as seeing Him who is invisible. ²⁸ By faith he kept the Passover and the sprinkling of blood, lest he who destroyed the firstborn should touch them. ²⁹ By faith they passed through the Red Sea as by dry land, whereas the Egyptians, attempting to do so, were drowned. ³⁰ By faith the walls of Jericho fell down after they were encircled for seven days. ³¹ By faith the harlot Rahab did not perish with those who did not believe, when she had received the spies with peace. ³² And what more shall I say? For the time would fail me to tell of Gideon and Barak and Samson and Jephthah, also of David and Samuel and the prophets: ³³ who through faith subdued kingdoms, worked righteousness, obtained promises, stopped the mouths of lions, ³⁴ quenched the violence of fire, escaped the edge of the sword, out of weakness were made strong, became valiant in battle, turned to flight the armies of the aliens. ³⁵ Women received their dead raised to life again. Others were tortured, not accepting deliverance, that they might obtain a better resurrection. ³⁶ Still others had trial of mockings and scourgings, yes, and of chains and imprisonment. ³⁷ They *were stoned, they were sawn in two, [k]were tempted, were slain with the sword. They wandered about in sheepskins and goatskins, being destitute, afflicted, tormented— 38 of whom the world was not worthy. They wandered in deserts and mountains, in dens and caves of the earth. 39 And all these, having obtained a good testimony through faith, did not receive the promise, 40 God having provided something better for us, that they should not be made perfect apart from us.*

Now, read the first two verses of Hebrews Chapter 12: *"Therefore we also, since we are surrounded by so great a cloud of witnesses, let us lay aside every weight, and the sin which so easily ensnares us, and let us run with endurance the race that is set before us, 2 looking unto Jesus, the author and finisher of our faith, who for the joy that was set before Him endured the cross, despising the shame, and has sat down at the right hand of the throne of God."*

Here, we are encouraged to run each race that is set before us with endurance, while laying aside every weight and the sin that so easily gets us off track. We are to keep our eyes on Jesus, who is the author and finisher of our faith. And if we ever feel ill-equipped for the race or the task we are about to undertake, all we have to do is call on the Father. He will hear our requests, and He will be there to provide our every need.

Furthermore, we must remember, the Word of God in Romans 4:17d that says, *"calleth those things which be not as though they were."* So, even with the task appears to be daunting and we become overwhelmed, we must not rely upon our own strength to carry us through. We can always call upon the Lord, and we can exercise the power and authority He has already given us.

Proverbs 18:21 says, *"Death and life are in the power of the tongue."* So, we can use our tongues to speak those things that be not as though they were, effectively calling them into being.

Chapter Three

Our Fight is Not in Vain

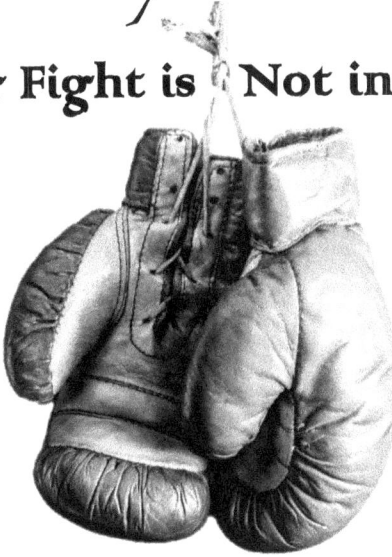

Unfortunately for people of color, injustices and prejudices are unconscionable evils that have been endured for far too long in the United States, beginning with the enslavement of Africans (in the early 1500s, prior to the Atlantic Slave Trade that began in the early 1600s) and failing to be extinguished even in present day life, some 500 years later. To our credit, many brave Black men and women have paved the way to a better life for us today than the ones through which our great grandparents, grandparents, and parents suffered. And, the struggles have definitely been arduous and numerous. And while we have made strides within the 500 hundred years of our time in this land, we have so very far to go to secure a safe future for our children, grandchildren, and great grandchildren.

To achieve our desired goal, we must stay in the press, keeping our eyes on the prize: true freedom, liberty, equality and equity in all areas in the land in which we reside. We are striving to make our mark, to demonstrate to the coming generations that the struggle is not yet over. There have been battles that have been won and many battles that have been lost, but the war is not yet over. So, onward we press!

Looking back through history can serve as an impetus to propel us forward. In this chapter, we will examine the road down which we have traveled, so we can determine the best path to take from here. There is much at stake, and we desire the best outcome for our collective future. To reach our desired goal, it is incumbent upon all of us to know how the journey began, so we can effectively complete the task at hand.

As we begin our journey into the past, let's start with a review of a set of laws that should have never been "instituted" after the abolishment of slavery, yet they did, and many suffered as a result of these statutes. Slaves having legally been "freed" did not experience true freedom under the law as they hoped they would, and Black Americans who had not experienced slavery were equally subjected to ill treatment.

Jim Crow Laws

Jim Crow laws were a collection of state and local statutes that legalized racial segregation. Named after a Black minstrel show character, the laws- which existed for about 100 years, from the post-Civil War era until 1968- were meant to marginalize African Americans by denying them the right to vote, hold jobs, get an education or other opportunities. Those who attempted to defy Jim Crow laws often faced arrest, fines, jail sentences, violence and death.

The roots of Jim Crow laws began as early as 1865, immediately following the ratification of the 13th Amendment, which abolished slavery in the United States.

Black codes were strict local and state laws that detailed when, where and how formerly enslaved people could work and for how much compensation. The codes appeared throughout the South as a legal way to put Black citizens into indentured servitude, to take voting rights away, to control where they lived, how they traveled, and to seize children for labor purposes.

The legal system was stacked against Black citizens, with former Confederate soldiers working as police and judges, making it difficult for African Americans to win court cases and ensuring they were subject to Black codes.

These codes worked in conjunction with labor camps for the incarcerated, where prisoners were treated as enslaved people. Black offenders typically received longer sentences than their white equals, and because of the grueling work, often did not live out their entire sentence. During the Reconstruction era, local governments, as well as the national Democratic Party and President Andrew Johnson, thwarted efforts to help Black Americans move forward.

Violence was on the rise, making danger a regular aspect of African American life. Black schools were vandalized and destroyed, and bands of violent white people attacked, tortured and lynched Black citizens in the night. Families were attacked and forced off their land all across the South.

The most ruthless organization of the Jim Crow era, the Ku Klux Klan, was born in 1865 in Pulaski, Tennessee, as a private club for Confederate veterans. The KKK grew into a secret society terrorizing Black communities and seeping through white Southern culture, with members at the highest levels of government and in the lowest echelons of criminal back alleys.

At the start of the 1880s, big cities in the South were not wholly beholden to Jim Crow laws and Black Americans found more freedom in them. This led to substantial Black populations moving to the cities and, as the decade progressed, white city dwellers demanded more laws to limit opportunities for African Americans.

Jim Crow laws soon spread around the country with even more force than previously. Public parks were forbidden for African Americans to enter, and theaters and restaurants were segregated. Segregated waiting rooms in bus and train stations were required, as well as water fountains, restrooms, building entrances, elevators, cemeteries, even amusement-park cashier windows.

Laws forbade African Americans from living in white neighborhoods. Segregation was enforced for public pools, phone booths, hospitals, asylums, jails and residential homes for the elderly and handicapped. Some states required separate textbooks for Black and white students.

New Orleans mandated the segregation of prostitutes according to race. In Atlanta, African Americans in court were given a different Bible from white people to swear on. Marriage and cohabitation between white and Black people were strictly forbidden in most Southern states. It was not uncommon to see signs posted at town and city limits warning African Americans that they were not welcome there.

As the 20th century progressed, Jim Crow laws flourished within an oppressive society marked by violence. Following World War I, the NAACP noted that lynchings had become so prevalent that it sent investigator Walter White to the South. White had lighter skin and could infiltrate white hate groups.

As lynchings increased, so did race riots, with at least 25 across the United States over several months in 1919, a period sometimes referred to as "Red Summer." In retaliation, white authorities charged Black communities with conspiring to conquer white America.

With Jim Crow dominating the landscape, education increasingly under attack and few opportunities for Black college graduates, the Great Migration of the 1920s saw a significant migration of educated Black people out of the South, spurred on by publications like The Chicago Defender, which encouraged Black Americans to move north. Read by millions of Southern Black people, white people attempted to ban the newspaper and threatened violence against any caught reading or distributing it.

The poverty of the Great Depression only deepened resentment, with a rise in lynchings, and after World War II, even Black veterans returning home met with segregation and violence.

The North was not immune to Jim Crow-like laws. Some states required Black people to own property before they could vote, schools and neighborhoods were segregated, and businesses displayed "Whites Only" signs.

In Ohio, segregationist Allen Granbery Thurman ran for governor in 1867 promising to bar Black citizens from voting. After he narrowly lost that political race, Thurman was appointed to the U.S. Senate, where he fought to dissolve Reconstruction-era reforms benefiting African Americans.

After World War II, suburban developments in the North and South were created with legal covenants that did not allow Black families, and Black people often found it difficult or impossible to obtain mortgages for homes in certain "red-lined" neighborhoods.

The post-World War II era saw an increase in civil rights activities in the African American community, with a focus on ensuring that Black citizens were able to vote. This ushered in the civil rights movement, resulting in the removal of Jim Crow laws.

In 1948 President Harry Truman ordered integration in the military, and in 1954, the Supreme Court ruled in Brown v. Board of Education that educational segregation was unconstitutional, bringing to an end the era of "separate-but-equal" education.

In 1964, President Lyndon B. Johnson signed the Civil Rights Act, which legally ended the segregation that had been institutionalized by Jim Crow laws. And in 1965, the Voting Rights Act halted efforts to keep minorities from voting. The Fair Housing Act of 1968, which ended discrimination in renting and selling homes, followed.

Jim Crow laws were technically off the books, though that has not always guaranteed full integration or adherence to anti-racism laws throughout the United States.

(History.com Editors. "Jim Crow Laws." February 18, 2018. History.com Accessed December 6, 2020.)

During the time Jim Crow Laws were alive and enforced, an organization emerged to effectuate change through the use of policy making and educational efforts. This organization has remained strong in its influence and is still in operation today with a reported strength of 500,000 members and growing.

National Association for the Advancement of Colored People (NAACP)

The National Association for the Advancement of Colored People (NAACP) was founded in 1909 as an interracial American organization that was created to work for the abolition of segregation and discrimination in housing, education, employment, voting, and transportation; to oppose racism; and to ensure African-Americans their constitutional rights. The NAACP was created by an interracial group consisting of W.E.B. Du Bois, Ida Bell Wells-Barnett, Mary White Ovington, and others concerned with the challenges facing African Americans, especially in the wake of the 1908 Springfield (Illinois) Race Riot.

Some of the founding members had been associated with the Niagara Movement, a civil rights group led by Du Bois.

Presented below is a timeline of notable events in which the NAACP was instrumental as the organization strives to rid our nation of injustices that stem from racial discrimination.

- 1909, Feb. 12 - The NAACP, the nation's oldest, largest, and most widely recognized grassroots-based civil rights organization is founded.
- 1917, July 1- Two white policemen were killed in East St. Louis, Ill. The incident sparked a race riot on July 2, which ended with 48 killed, hundreds injured, and thousands of blacks fleeing the city when their homes were burned. On July 28, the NAACP protested with a silent march of 10,000 black men, women, and children down New York's Fifth Avenue.
- 1919 - The most savage and brutal example of white supremacy was a lynch mob. In 1919 the NAACP published a landmark report, "Thirty Years of Lynching in the United States: 1889-1918." The report was the foundation used to end this brutal form of political and economic terrorism.
- 1922, April 20 - Anti - lynching Bill; It was intended to establish lynching as a federal crime. The Dyer Anti-Lynching Bill was re-introduced in subsequent sessions of Congress and passed by the U.S. House of Representatives on January 26, 1922, but its passage was halted in the Senate by a filibuster by Southern Democrats, who formed a powerful block. To this date, the bill still has not become law, after over 200 attempts, but great strides have been made in 2020 with the bill being passed in the House of Representatives.

- 1940, March 20 - Thurgood Marshall founded the NAACP Legal Defense and Educational Fund.
- 1948 - The NAACP's Washington, D.C. bureau helped advance the integration of the armed forces.
- 1954 - NAACP Litigation Director Charles Hamilton Houston and its Legal Counsel, Thurgood Marshall, fought 26 cases before the Supreme Court, none more important than Brown v. Board of Education. Brown v. Board is one of the major legal landmarks guaranteeing the right to equality in American society. Education is the key to full citizenship.
- 1957 - Helped advance the Civil Rights Act
- 1963 - March on Washington
- 1965 - The passage of the Civil Rights Act of 1964 and the Voting Rights Act of 1965 during President Johnson's administration were milestone achievements, and the NAACP's role in these victories cannot be minimized. The Voting Rights Act of 1965 provided direct federal enforcement to remove literacy tests and other devices that had been used to disenfranchise African Americans.
- 1989, Aug. 26 - the NAACP sponsored a symbolic silent march in Washington, D.C., to protest recent adverse Supreme Court decisions on affirmative action and minorities set-asides. The march was modeled on the historic 1917 New York City silent march protesting the East St. Louis Riot against unfair voting practices. Accordingly, the more than 100,000 participants dressed in black and white, marched behind a row of drummers from a rally on the National Mall to the U.S. Capitol.
- 2000 - After the 2000 presidential election, the NAACP received numerous complaints about voter irregularities in Florida. On Jan. 10, 2001, the NAACP joined other organizations to file a class action lawsuit on behalf of

thousands of voters against Florida Secretary of State Katherine Harris, Director of the Florida Division of Elections Clay Roberts, and Georgia Corporation Database Technologies for unfair voting practices.
("NAACP Timeline." sutori.com and thoughtsco.com. Reviewed December 2020.)

In the midst of the accomplishments gained by the NAACP, many individuals were led by an internal charge to join the cause of gaining true freedom, respect, and rights for Black Americans. These individuals included Rosa Parks, Dr. Martin Luther King, Jr., Malcom X, Huey Newton, Senator John Lewis, Medgar Evers, Senator Barbara Jordan, Stokely Carmichael, Rev. Jesse Jackson, Nelson Mandela, W.E.B. Du Bois, Thurgood Marshall, Rev. Fred Shuttlesworth, and Desmond Tutu, amongst a host of many others. They participated in what became known as one of the most momentous movements in the history of the United States.

Civil Rights Movement of the 1950s – 1960s
The American Civil Rights Movement was a time of great momentum and change for Black Americans, as leaders stood tall and lifted their voices and their pens to effectuate changes that had never been made before. In doing so, many of them were arrested, some served jail sentences, and some lost their lives fighting for the cause.

Presented on the next several pages is a timeline of major events that occurred during that great era.

1954 – *Brown vs. Board of Education*
- This event is one of the most significant trials in US history.
- Segregation of White and Black Children - This supreme court case ended segregation in the classroom

- Brown Vs. the Board of Education Historic Site - Learn about where the injustice behind this court case took place.

1955 – *Montgomery Bus Boycott*

- Montgomery Bus Boycott - Articles, historical timelines and biographies of important people who made the Montgomery Bus Boycott a critical piece of US history.
- Rosa Parks - One of the most famous people to come out of the Civil rights movement, Rosa Parks was a key factor in the Montgomery Bus Boycott.
- Martin Luther King, Jr. - The face of the Civil Rights Movement, Martin Luther King, Jr. helped to lead the Montgomery Bus Boycott.

1957 – *Desegregation at Little Rock*

- Segregation Showdown at Little Rock - Follow the archives through the breakdown of segregation in Little Rock, Arkansas.
- Little Rock Central High School - The protest of black students entering this Arkansas school got so bad, President Eisenhower was forced to send in federal protection.

1960 – *Sit-in Campaign*

- Sit-in Campaign - The basis of sit-in campaigns resulted from students "sitting" at lunch counters until they were acknowledged and served food.
- Nashville, TN Sit-in Campaigns - African Americans would sit and wait at the lunch counters in a very polite, non-violent manner. If police arrested them for not leaving, a new group of African Americans would take their place.

1961 – *Freedom Rides*

- Civil Rights Movements and Freedom Rides - Learn how American's tested the commitment to Civil rights through this unique strategy.
- Freedom Riders - The Congress on Racial Equality organized these techniques by placing black and white volunteers next to each other on buses and other forms of public transportation.
- Freedom Rides - See how the freedom riders played a part in the Civil rights movement timeline.

1962 – *Mississippi Riot*

- Mississippi Riot of Mississippi rallied against a federal court's decision to allow one black man to attend an all-white school.
- James H. Meredith - This man was a crucial figure in the American Civil rights movement. By having a federal court approve his case to attend an all-white school in Mississippi, riots broke out and in turn paved the way for equality in the US.

1963 – *Birmingham*

- Birmingham Demonstrations - Read about the efforts Martin Luther King Jr. and citizens hoping for change took to ensure equality for all.
- Birmingham Civil Rights District - A historical look at all of the events that took place in Birmingham during the Civil rights movement.

1963 – *March on Washington*

- March on Washington - With an estimated 250,000 people in attendance, this was truly a landmark event for the Civil rights movement.

- March on Washington for Jobs and Freedom - Both black and white people gathered together to witness Martin Luther King, Jr. give his historical "I Have a Dream" speech.
- "I Have a Dream" - by Martin Luther King, Jr. His awe-inspiring words united a nation.

1964 – *Freedom Summer*

- In the summer of 1964, forty-one Freedom Schools opened in the churches, on the back porches, and under the trees of Mississippi.
- Mississippi Freedom Summer (Summer Project) Events

1965 – *Selma*

- Bloody Sunday - The demonstration march from Selma to Montgomery was nicknamed "Bloody Sunday" due to the brutality and violence troops used against the peaceful demonstrators.
- March 7th Selma, Alabama - Over 600 people partook in the March from Selma, Alabama.

("American Civil Rights" www.gettysburgflag.com/timeline-american-civil-rights. Retrieved December 1, 2020.)

Prior to the Civil Rights Movement, action was taken in the courts, impacting all 50 states, to institute equality in hiring practices and educational opportunities. These laws began during the Reconstruction Era (1863-1877), continued through the Civil Rights movement on into present day although not all states continue to recognize the action as a matter of law.

Affirmative Action

Affirmative action in the United States is a set of laws, policies, guidelines, and administrative practices "intended to end and correct the effects of a specific form of discrimination" that include government-mandated, government-approved, and voluntary private programs. The programs tend to focus on access to education and employment, granting special consideration to historically excluded groups, specifically racial minorities or women. The impetus toward affirmative action is redressing the disadvantages associated with past and present discrimination. Further impetus is a desire to ensure public institutions, such as universities, hospitals, and police forces, are more representative of the populations they serve.

In the United States, affirmative action included the use of racial quotas until the Supreme Court ruled that quotas were unconstitutional. Affirmative action currently tends to emphasize not specific quotas but rather "targeted goals" to address past discrimination in a particular institution or in broader society through "good-faith efforts ... to identify, select, and train potentially qualified minorities and women."

For example, many higher education institutions have voluntarily adopted policies which seek to increase recruitment of racial   minorities. Outreach campaigns,   targeted recruitment, employee and management development, and employee support programs are examples of affirmative action in employment. Ten states in the US have banned affirmative action: California (1996), Texas (1996), Washington (1998), Florida (1999), Michigan (2006), Nebraska (2008), Arizona (2010), New Hampshire (2012), Oklahoma (2012), and Idaho (2020). However, Texas's ban with *Hopwood v. Texas* was reversed in 2003 by *Grutter v. Bollinger*, leaving nine states that currently ban the policy.

Affirmative action policies were developed to address long histories of discrimination faced by minorities and women, which reports suggest produced corresponding unfair advantages for whites and males. They first emerged from debates over non-discrimination policies in the 1940s and during the civil rights movement. These debates led to federal executive orders requiring non-discrimination in the employment policies of some government agencies and contractors in the 1940s and onward, and to Title VII of the Civil Rights Act of 1964 which prohibited racial discrimination in firms with over 25 employees.

The first federal policy of race-conscious affirmative action was the Revised Philadelphia Plan, implemented in 1969, which required certain government contractors to set "goals and time-tables" for integrating and diversifying their workforce. Similar policies emerged through a mix of voluntary practices and federal and state policies in employment and education. Affirmative action as a practice was partially upheld by the Supreme Court in *Grutter v. Bollinger* (2003), while the use of racial quotas for college admissions was concurrently ruled unconstitutional by the Court in *Gratz v. Bollinger* (2003).

Affirmative action often gives rise to controversy in American politics. Supporters argue that affirmative action is still needed to counteract continuing bias and prejudice against women and minorities. Opponents argue that these policies amount to discrimination against other minorities, such as Asian Americans, which entails favoring one group over another based upon racial preference rather than achievement, and many believe that the diversity of current American society suggests that affirmative action policies succeeded and are no longer required. Supporters point to contemporary examples of conscious and unconscious biases, such as the finding that job-seekers with black-sounding names may be less likely to get a callback than those with white-sounding names, as proof that affirmative action is not obsolete.

So, what lead to the change from states operating in agreement with Affirmative Action policies? In 1983, Reagan signed

Executive Order 12432, which instructed government agencies to create a development plan for Minority Business Enterprises. While the Reagan administration opposed discriminatory practices, it did not support the implementation of it in the form of quotas and goals (Executive Order 11246). Bi-partisan opposition in Congress and other government officials blocked the repeal of this Executive Order. Reagan was particularly known for his opposition to affirmative action programs. He reduced funding for the Equal Employment Opportunity Commission, arguing that "reverse discrimination" resulted from these policies. However, the courts reaffirmed affirmative action policies such as quotas. In 1986, the Supreme Court ruled that courts could order race-based quotas to fight discrimination in worker unions in *Sheet Metal Workers' International Association v. EEOC*, 478 U.S. 42. In 1987, in *Johnson v. Transportation Agency, Santa Clara County, California*, 480 U.S. 616, the Supreme Court ruled that sex or race was a factor that could be considered in a pool of qualified candidates by employers.

Similar to the longevity of Affirmative Action and the NAACP, a pair of individuals collaborated and formed an organization that would operate for nearly two decades and persevere during times of adversity and exist despite gaining the label 'militant' because of their tactics. Regardless of the 'militant' label, this organization of die-hard individuals would not be swayed to look the other way when police brutality towards Black Americans reared its ugly head. They stood firm in their convictions and were not afraid to let others know who they were and what they stood for. This organization was a demonstration of strength in action as they sought to impact our nation by bringing an end to police brutality, while ushering in equality for Black Americans in the realms of housing and employment.

Black Panthers

The Black Panthers, also known as the Black Panther Party, was a political organization founded in 1966 by Huey Newton and Bobby Seale to challenge police brutality against the African American community. Dressed in black berets and black leather jackets, the Black Panthers organized armed citizen patrols of Oakland and other U.S. cities. At its peak in 1968, the Black Panther Party had roughly 2,000 members. The organization later declined as a result of internal tensions, deadly shootouts and FBI counterintelligence activities aimed at weakening the organization.

Black Panther Party founders Huey Newton and Bobby Seale met in 1961 while students at Merritt College in Oakland, California. They both protested the college's "Pioneer Day" celebration, which honored the pioneers who came to California in the 1800s, but omitted the role of African Americans in settling the American West. Seale and Newton formed the Negro History Fact Group, which called on the school to offer classes in black history.

They founded the Black Panthers in the wake of the assassination of black nationalist Malcolm X and after police in San Francisco shot and killed an unarmed black teen named Matthew Johnson.

Originally dubbed the Black Panther Party for Self-Defense, the organization was founded in October 1966. The Black Panthers' early activities primarily involved monitoring police activities in black communities in Oakland and other cities.

As they instituted a number of social programs and engaged in political activities, their popularity grew. The Black Panthers drew widespread support from urban centers with large minority communities, including Los Angeles, Chicago, New York and Philadelphia. By 1968, the Black Panthers had roughly 2,000 members across the country.

Newton and Seale drew on Marxist ideology for the party platform. They outlined the organization's philosophical views and political objectives in a Ten-Point Program.

The Ten-Point Program called for an immediate end to police brutality; employment for African Americans; and land, housing and justice for all.

The Black Panthers were part of the larger Black Power movement, which emphasized black pride, community control and unification for civil rights.

While the Black Panthers were often portrayed as a gang, their leadership saw the organization as a political party whose goal was getting more African Americans elected to political office. They were unsuccessful on this front. By the early 1970s, FBI counterintelligence efforts, criminal activities and an internal rift between group members weakened the party as a political force.

The Black Panthers did, however, start a number of popular community social programs, including free breakfast programs for school children and free health clinics in 13 African American communities across the United States.

The Black Panthers were involved in numerous violent encounters with police. In 1967, founder Huey Newton allegedly killed Oakland police officer John Frey. Newton was convicted of voluntary manslaughter in 1968 and was sentenced to two to 15 years in prison. An appellate court decision later reversed the conviction.

Eldridge Cleaver, editor of the Black Panther's newspaper, and 17-year old Black Panther member and treasurer Bobby Hutton, were involved in a shootout with police in 1968 that left Hutton dead and two police officers wounded.

Conflicts within the party often turned violent too. In 1969, Black Panther Party member Alex Rackley was tortured and murdered by other Black Panthers who thought him a police informant.

Black Panther bookkeeper Betty Van Patter was found beaten and murdered in 1974. No one was charged with the death, though many believed that party leadership was responsible.

The Black Panthers' socialist message and black nationalist focus made them the target of a secret FBI counterintelligence program called COINTELPRO.

In 1969, the FBI declared the Black Panthers a communist organization and an enemy of the United States government. The first FBI's first director, J. Edgar Hoover, in 1968 called the Black Panthers, "One of the greatest threats to the nation's internal security."

The FBI worked to weaken the Panthers by exploiting existing rivalries between black nationalist groups. They also worked to undermine and dismantle the Free Breakfast for Children Program and other community social programs instituted by the Black Panthers.

In 1969, Chicago police gunned down and killed Black Panther Party members Fred Hampton and Mark Clark, who were asleep in their apartment.

About a hundred bullets were fired in what police described as a fierce gun battle with members of the Black Panther Party. However, ballistics experts later determined that only one of those bullets came from the Panthers' side.

Although the FBI was not responsible for leading the raid, a federal grand jury later indicated that the bureau played a significant role in the events leading up to the raid. The Black Panther Party officially dissolved in 1982.

The New Black Panther Party is a black nationalist organization founded in Dallas, Texas, in 1989. Members of the original Black Panther Party say there's no relation between the New Black Panther Party and the original Black Panthers.

The United States Commission on Civil Rights and the Southern Poverty Law Center have called the New Black Panther Party a hate group. ("Black Panthers" History.com Editors. www.history.com. November 3, 2017. Accessed on December 7, 2020.)

While the Black Panthers may not have been successful during their existence in their attempts to expand the presence of Black Americans in politics, over time, their plight along with those who participated in the Civil Rights Movement would prove to be worthwhile. Finally, after much bloodshed, sweat, and an abundance of tears, change would be effectuated in a magnanimous way in the political arena with the election of the first African American president approximately thirty years later.

President Barack Obama

Barack Hussein Obama II (born August 4, 1961) is an American politician and attorney who served as the 44th president of the United States from 2009 to 2017. A member of the Democratic Party, Obama was the first African-American president of the United States. He previously served as a U.S. senator from Illinois from 2005 to 2008 and an Illinois state senator from 1997 to 2004.

Obama was born in Honolulu, Hawaii. After graduating from Columbia University in 1983, he worked as a community organizer in Chicago. In 1988, he enrolled in Harvard Law School, where he was the first black person to be president of the *Harvard Law Review*. After graduating, he became a civil rights attorney and an academic, teaching constitutional law at the University of Chicago Law School from 1992 to 2004. Turning to elective politics, he represented the 13th district from 1997 until 2004 in the Illinois Senate, when he ran for the U.S. Senate. Obama received national attention in 2004 with his March Senate primary

win, his well-received July Democratic National Convention keynote address, and his landslide November election to the
Senate.

In 2008, he was nominated for president a year after his
presidential campaign began, and after a close primary campaign
against Hillary Clinton, Obama was elected over Republican John
McCain and was inaugurated alongside Joe Biden on January 20,
2009. Nine months later, he was named the 2009 Nobel Peace
Prize laureate.

Obama signed many landmark bills into law during his first
two years in office. The main reforms that were passed include
the *Affordable Care Act* (commonly referred to as ACA or
"Obamacare"), although without a public health insurance option,
the *Dodd–Frank Wall Street Reform and Consumer Protection Act,*
and the *Don't Ask, Don't Tell Repeal Act* of 2010. *The American
Recovery and Reinvestment Act* of 2009 and Tax Relief,
Unemployment Insurance Reauthorization, and *Job Creation Act* of
2010 served as economic stimuli amidst the Great Recession.

After a lengthy debate over the national debt limit, he signed
the *Budget Control and the American Taxpayer Relief Acts.* In
foreign policy, he increased U.S. troop levels in Afghanistan,
reduced nuclear weapons with the United States–Russia New
START treaty, and ended military involvement in the Iraq War. He
ordered military involvement in Libya for the implementation of
the UN Security Council Resolution 1973, contributing to the
overthrow of Muammar Gaddafi. He also ordered the military
operations that resulted in the deaths of Osama bin Laden and
suspected Yemeni Al-Qaeda operative Anwar al-Awlaki.

After winning re-election by defeating Rep. opponent Mitt
Romney, Obama was sworn in for a second term in 2013. During
this term, he promoted inclusion for LGBT+ Americans. His
administration filed briefs that urged the Supreme Court to strike
down same-sex marriage bans as unconstitutional (*United States*

v. Windsor and *Obergefell v. Hodges*); same-sex marriage was legalized nationwide in 2015 after the Court ruled so in *Obergefell*. He advocated for gun control in response to the Sandy Hook Elementary School shooting, indicating support for a ban on assault weapons, and issued wide-ranging executive actions concerning global warming and immigration.

In foreign policy, he ordered military intervention in Iraq in response to gains made by ISIL after the 2011 withdrawal from Iraq, continued the process of ending U.S. combat operations in Afghanistan in 2016, promoted discussions that led to the 2015 Paris Agreement on global climate change, initiated sanctions against Russia following the invasion in Ukraine and again after Russian interference in the 2016 United States elections, brokered the JCPOA nuclear deal with Iran, and normalized U.S. relations with Cuba.

Obama nominated three justices to the Supreme Court: Sonia Sotomayor and Elena Kagan were confirmed as justices, while Merrick Garland faced partisan obstruction from the Republican-led Senate, which never held hearings or a vote on the nomination.

During Obama's term in office, the United States' reputation abroad, as well as the American economy, significantly improved. His presidency has generally been regarded favorably, and evaluations of his presidency among historians, political scientists, and the general public frequently place him among the upper tier of American presidents, specifically in the second quartile. Obama left office in January 2017 and continues to reside in Washington, D.C.

("President Barack Obama." The White House. 2008. Archived from the original on October 26, 2009. Reviewed December 2020.)

Although most Black Americans (certainly not all) celebrated President Barack Obama's success in the 2008 election and his eight-year tenure from 2009-2017, there is still so much to learn, understand and know about his journey, for we are on the outside looking into his world.

Here is something I learned while reading *A Promised Land* (2020) by Barack Obama, a novel in which he shares life as an Illinois state senator, a United States Senator, his journey to and through the presidency, and many perceptions about varying topics. This quote is taken directly from the novel:

> I had been assigned Secret Service protection in May 2007, just a few months after my campaign began- given the code name "Renegade" and a round-the-clock security detail. This wasn't the norm. Unless you were a sitting vice president (or, in the case of Hillary, a former First Lady), candidates typically weren't assigned coverage until they'd all but secured the nomination. The reason my case was handled differently, the reason Harry Reid and Bernie Thompson, chair of the House Homeland Security Committee, had publicly insisted the Service move early, was straightforward. The number of threats directed my way exceeded anything the Secret Service had ever seen before.
>
> ...to suddenly have armed men and women hovering around me wherever I went, posted outside every room I occupied, was a shock to my system. My view of the outside world started to shift, obscured by the veil of security. I no longer walked through the front entrance of a building when a back stairwell was available. If I worked out in a hotel gym, agents first covered the windows with cloth to prevent a potential shooter from getting a sight line. Bulletproof barriers were placed inside any room I slept in, including our bedroom at home in Chicago. And I no longer had the option of driving myself anywhere, not even around the block. (p. 136-7)

Reading his words immediately brought tears to my eyes. Then, imagining how he must have felt during that time of his life broke my heart, knowing the tremendous grief he bore. Not only did his reality hurt, but also the reality of the continued existence of bigotry, degradation, hatred, discrimination and racism Black Americans still endure in this day and age was devastating to read. Why would some people hate Blacks so much that they could not stand to see one serve in the highest office of this land? What makes us so unworthy of such an honor in some people's eyes that they would want to take our lives? The realization of the depth of people's hatred and dislike for us is disheartening.

During Obama's presidency, I had heard about the threats on his life, and I prayed heartily that he and his family would not be harmed. Now, each time I see him on television, sharing with the world his wisdom, I am thankful that he is still breathing and safe. Through all of that, I had never heard him share his personal experiences with the threats and how greatly they had impacted his life, and to now read it in his book, really opens a personal world of insight that one could have only wondered about until now.

Thank God for President Obama's bravery, because he could have thrown in the towel a long time ago. Praise God for his strength and endurance to run the race and not allow anyone to deter him or undermine is rights as an American citizen. Thank God for President Obama's audacity to hope.

Following President Barack Obama's presidency, although the nation was still in need of much improvement in areas across the board, we, as a country, had made great strides comparative to the prior presidential time periods.

Unfortunately, during President Obama's tenure, police shootings involving African Americans was on the rise. Conversely, shootings of police officers in retaliation for lives lost was also on the rise. This social disruption gave rise to yet another movement in an attempt to stabilize our society within the relations of police and citizen relations.

Black Lives Matter Movement (BLM)

The Black Lives Matter Movement campaigns against violence and systemic racism towards Black people. The international human rights campaign began on social media in 2013 with the #BlackLivesMatter hashtag and has since gone on to lead calls for Black people to be treated fairly by authorities in the USA and around the world.

According to Black Lives Matter, the movement is "an ideological and political intervention in a world where Black lives are systematically and intentionally targeted for demise. It is an affirmation of Black folks' humanity, our contributions to this society, and our resilience in the face of deadly oppression." In 2018, five years after Black Lives Matter began, co-founder Alicia Garza said in an interview that BLM's "goal is to build the kind of society where black people can live with dignity and respect." (Turan, Cyan. June 19, 2020. cosmopolitan.com. Reviewed December 1, 2020.)

Here is the annual timeline for the Black Lives Matter Movement, demonstrating key details and actions of its members and participants.

2013 - The Black Lives Matter movement began in 2013, following the death of Trayvon Martin, an African-American teenager who was shot while walking to a family friend's house, and the subsequent acquittal of George Zimmerman, the man who shot him.

The campaign was co-founded by three Black women: Alicia Garza, Patrisse Cullors, and Opal Tometi, as a response to the police killings of Black people. The phrase "black lives matter" was first used in a Facebook post by Garza after Zimmerman was found not guilty and was the inspiration for the campaign. Cullors recognized the power of Garza's words and created the hashtag #BlackLivesMatter, and the campaign was born.

2014 - The movement quickly gathered pace, with interest and momentum spiking every time a Black person was killed as a result of an altercation with police.

In 2014, Black Lives Matter protested against the deaths of numerous Black and African-American people. In July that year, Eric Garner died in New York City after a policeman put him in a chokehold while arresting him. Then, in August, unarmed teenager Michael Brown was killed by a gunshot from a police officer, Darren Wilson (it was later decided that there was not enough evidence to charge Wilson). Both peaceful protests and riots followed, much of which was done under the banner and hashtag of Black Lives Matter.

In response, co-founder Patrisse Cullors organized the Black Life Matters Ride, which drew a gathering of 600 people and sparked the founding of more localized Black Lives Matter groups and the dissemination of the campaign into a network.

2015 - The following year saw another spate of Black people killed by police officers in the USA, including Walter Scott, Freddie Gray, and Meagan Hockaday. Black Lives Matter protested against these and many more. They also organized protests to highlight the injustices faced by Black women and Black transgender women. By the end of 2015, 21 transgender people had been killed that year in the USA, a record number at the time, and 13 of the victims were Black.

2016 - 2016 saw Black Lives Matter organize many more protests against police brutality towards Black people. Those whose deaths occurred due to police actions included Deborah Danner and Alton Sterling. Early July saw over 100 protests take place across America following Sterling's death on July 5th, and Philandro Castile's shooting the next day.

This year also saw major American sports stars lend their voices to the cause of Black Lives Matter. In July 2016, basketball players, including LeBron James and Carmelo Anthony, opened an awards ceremony by speaking about recent deaths of Black people, saying: "Enough is enough." Then, from August, many sports stars began taking part in protests during national anthems at sports games, beginning with Colin Kaepernick, who knelt during the anthem ahead of an NFL game.

2017 - Black History Month is celebrated in February in the USA (it's marked in October in the UK). In 2017, Black Lives Matter put on their first art exhibition timed to coincide with Black History Month in the US state of Virginia. It featured the work of over 30 Black artists and creators.

Black Lives Matter protest not only the killings of Black people, but also some acquittals and 'not guilty' verdicts in those cases which make it to trial. In June, they held a protest after the officer accused of killing Philandro Castile the year before was found not guilty.

In August, Black Lives Matter campaigners were among counter-protestors at a white supremacist 'Unite the Right' rally in Charlottesville, Virginia.

2018 - In an interview with ABC News marking five years of Black Lives Matter, Cullors explained the impact the organization had had on other causes. She said: "[BLM] has popularized civil disobedience and the need to put our bodies on the line... With things like the Women's March, and Me Too, and March for our Lives, all of these movements, their foundations are in Black Lives Matter."

By May 1, 2018, a study found that #BlackLivesMatter had been used nearly 30 million times on Twitter since the first instance in 2013.

As they marked five years of action, Black Lives Matter continued to highlight the deaths of Black people who had lost their lives at the hands of US police that year, including Grechario Mack and Kenneth Ross, Jr.

2019 - In February 2019, the rapper 21 Savage was arrested and detained by the US's immigration agency, ICE. As a result, Cullors convened a group of 60 high profile stars from the music and entertainment worlds to advocate for his release.

Then, in May, Oklahoma teenager Isaiah Lewis was shot by police and killed. Days later, Black Lives Matter held a 100-strong rally in protest.

2020 - Major protests were sparked at the end of May following the death of George Floyd in Minneapolis. A video showing a police officer kneeling on Floyd's neck went viral following his death. Police officer, Derek Chauvin, has since been charged with second-degree murder - raised from an initial charge of third-degree murder and second-degree manslaughter (the case is yet to go to trial). Three other officers who were there have all been charged with aiding and abetting second-degree murder and aiding and abetting second-degree manslaughter. Their cases are also yet to go to trial.

Black Lives Matter went on to organize protests around the world. In London, two Black activists Aima, 18, and Tash, 21, organized a rally in Trafalgar Square, which was attended by thousands on Sunday, May 31st.

Many more have followed since. At one London protest, *Star Wars* actor John Boyega joined 15,000 others in Hyde Park, and told crowds:

"Today is about innocent people who were halfway through their process, we don't know what George Floyd could have achieved, we don't know what Sandra Bland could have achieved, but today we're going to make sure that won't be an alien thought to our young ones."

(Turan, Cyan. June 19, 2020. cosmopolitan.com. Reviewed December 1, 2020.)

In addition to all of the movements and the legal advancements made in education, employment, and housing, there were several specific court cases that were decided in favor of Black Americans as a unit, providing equality under the law- to be recognized in all states. Regrettably, some court case rulings were against the advancement of Blacks. Summarized below are two landmark cases with negative outcomes, four landmark cases with favorable outcomes, and two executive orders that changed history from the mid-nineteenth century to the twentieth century.

Court Cases and Executive Orders

Dred Scott v. Sandford (1857)

In Dred Scott v. Sandford, the Supreme Court ruled that Americans of African descent, whether free or slave, were not American citizens and could not sue in federal court. The Court also ruled that Congress lacked power to ban slavery in the U.S. territories. Finally, the Court declared that the rights of slaveowners were constitutionally protected by the Fifth Amendment because slaves were categorized as property.

Plessy v. Ferguson (1896)

In this case, the Supreme Court upheld a Louisiana law requiring railroads to separate blacks and whites into different passenger cars. The Court affirmed the idea that the races could be segregated by law as long as the public facilities available to each race were "equal, but separate."

Brown v. Board of Education of Topeka, Kansas (1954)

Brown v. Board of Education of Topeka was a landmark 1954 Supreme Court case in which the justices ruled unanimously that racial segregation of children in public schools was unconstitutional.

Brown v. Board of Education of Topeka II, Kansas (1955)

In 1955, the Supreme Court considered arguments by the schools requesting relief concerning the task of desegregation. In their decision, the court delegated the task of carrying out school desegregation to district courts with orders that desegregation occur "with all deliberate speed."

Loving v. Virginia (1967)

Loving v. Virginia is a landmark civil rights decision of the United States Supreme Court, which invalidated laws prohibiting interracial marriage.

Swann v. Charlotte-Mecklenburg Board of Education (1971)

Swann v. Charlotte-Mecklenburg Board of Education was a landmark United States Supreme Court case dealing with the busing of students to promote integration in public schools.

Executive Order 10590 (1955)

On January 15 President Dwight D. Eisenhower signs Executive Order 10590 which creates the President's Committee on Government Policy to enforce the federal government's policy of nondiscrimination in federal employment.

Executive Order 10925 (1961)

Executive Order 10925, required government contractors to "take affirmative action to ensure that applicants are employed and that employees are treated during employment without regard to their race, creed, color, or national origin.

(MSU Billings Library. "African-American Rights Movements: Legislation / Court Cases." https://libguides.msubillings.edu. December 5, 2019. Accessed December 6, 2020.)

Having examined and reminded ourselves of the rich and eventful past of the plight of Black Americans, we are now well prepared to examine the conditions of life as they exist today.

Chapter Four

Tearing Down the Work

I am going to warn you now that this chapter may not be easy to read giving the level of truth that is within it, but the truth - the reality check - is needed if we are going to move forward as a people. Without truth and self-examination, we will literally get nowhere. There will be no growth or improvement. And, because I believe the desires and goals we have as a people are attainable, we must stop and have a reality check in order to move forward in achieving them.

If you have read most of my books, then you know I whole-heartedly believe in taking time out for self-examinations. They are necessary to determine whether or not goals are reachable according to the condition of the present circum-stances. So, while the words contained in this chapter may be uncomfortable to read, it is a necessary 'evil' that must occur. So, bear with me, and let's take it all in.

Before I begin, allow me to once again give you the Word of God from Hosea 4:6: *"My people are destroyed for lack of know-ledge: because thou hast rejected knowledge, I will also reject thee, that thou shalt be no priest to me: seeing thou hast forgotten the law of thy God, I will also forget thy children."* When we do not possess the vital information (knowledge) necessary for attaining our desired outcomes, we will fall prey to those who conspire against us, while unknowingly walking into snares. Snares are set to entrap us, preventing us from attaining our desired goals. Obtaining wisdom will assist us in attaining all we have in our sights.

While keeping Hosea 4:6 in the forefront of your mind, we are ready to move forward. Read this scenario: Monica, an African American teenage girl, walks into a classroom at the local high school and takes a seat. Behind her, the whispers begin as a few of her peers (Sonia, Tonya, and Keisha) begin their daily banter of ridicule with Monica as their target for the day. As they survey her, they talk about the natural tight curls of her hair and the deep mocha color of her skin. Having her rich complexion and hair textured ridiculed is nothing new for Monica. She has heard it most days of her life while being in public and even at her elementary school and junior high school, from a young child up to her teenage years. However, what surprises her most of all about the situation is this is the first time she experiences such disdain from members of her own race. Inside, she hurts, and she quickly brushes a tear from her eye before anyone notices.

As stated in the scenario, Monica had experienced discrimination and ridicule due to her physical appearance with most of the comments coming from those outside her race. In the United States and most parts of the world, beauty has been equated with fair skin, blonde hair, and blue eyes. This definition of beauty was and is still well defined in the media in television shows, commercials, advertisements, etc. With this idea of beauty being perpetuated for centuries, it has become ingrained in the minds of many people, regardless of their race.

To hear one person of a particular race make derogatory comments about the physical features of a person of a different race is not surprising. It has been done for so long that we have pretty much accepted that people prefer their own kind as they only seem to appreciate or prefer beauty that equates to features they possess. That is, of course, not to say that people cannot see the beauty of others who are different from them. Of course, they can. That is not the point here. The point is people don't usually equate people of other races as being beautiful as they would for someone who looks more like them. So, discrimination between the races based on a person's looks has unfortunately become common place.

In reference to the scenario you just read, what may be surprising to some is the incident of ridicule that was taking place among this group of African American teenage girls, with one girl being teased by three others about her physical features.

Well, the reality is physical features (hair texture, skin tone, shape of nose) are not the only cause of teasing and ridicule that is done amongst people of the same race. People often ridicule people about their speech patterns. For example, if a person does not utilize slang or broken speech but instead uses Standard English, he/she is referred to as "speaking white," as though it is the going thing to use broken English. Somehow, using correct sentence structure has come to be a white thing rather than just being correct.

Others are ridiculed when they reside in an upscale neighborhood versus living in a poorer one and vice versa. People are actually judged based on where they reside. Others are discriminated against due to their scholastic achievements. Unfortunately, the higher one excels in his/her educational pursuits, he/she is seen as different. And, different does not always have a positive connotation.

Do the examples I have illustrated here qualify as racism or discrimination? Can someone actually be racist against someone of his/her same race? Unfortunately, the answer is yes, and this type of racism is more prevalent than we may want to admit. The term to describe the racism described here, when a person of one race discriminates against another person of his/her own race, is intraracial racism and discrimination. And, in most cases, the origin of intraracial tension can be traced for each race.

For African Americans, where and when did intraracial discrimination originate? From my research and also substantiated by the 2014 research of social scientist Christopher Busey of Kent State University, "intraracial discrimination is one of many ugly legacies of slavery and plantation politics in which intentional intraracial division was established on plantations by slave owners in the form of color codes."

"These color codes then served as the basis for a hierarchy within the Black race in which mulattos and lighter-skinned Blacks found themselves in more 'favorable' and privileged positions on plantations" (Busey, 2014). These color codes, which led to favorable and privileged positions, is what contributed to the existence of the "house slave" and the "field slave." During the time of slavery, slaves either worked inside the slave owner's house or outside in the field.

"The process of turning a person into a house [slave] or field [slave] was called 'seasoning.' The goal of seasoning was to socialize the enslaved into disciplined, obedient workers. The practice itself was coercive and extremely violent. The central task was to remove the cultural memory of those enslaved to ensure that notions of African inferiority and white superiority could replace it within three years" (Encyclopedia.com "House Slaves an Overview." 2019. Accessed December 9, 2020).

"During the seasoning process, [slaves] were divided into three categories: New Africans or saltwater Negroes; Old Africans; and Creoles. New Africans or saltwater Negroes represented those recently from Africa. They spoke indigenous languages, carried African names, and maintained a strong connection to the culture of their ancestors. They were often considered the most dangerous and prone to rebellion. Old Africans were those who were born in Africa but spent a considerable amount of time within the plantation system. Typically, they were middle-aged and elderly persons. Creoles were persons of African descent who were born in the Americas. Their social experiences were limited to the culture of American slave plantations. For the most part Creoles and Old Africans were preferred as house servants" (Encyclopedia.com "House Slaves an Overview." 2019. Accessed December 9, 2020).

What is not stated here is that the Creole slaves are mostly, if not entirely, as result of intercourse between slaves and the slave owners, which were in most cases, but certainly not all, a result of sexual assault: rape. These rapes often produced interracial offspring, with the children having lineage not only to Africa but to Europe as well.

Creoles typically have lighter skin and were therefore preferred by the slave owners and chosen to be house slaves. This system of choosing based on skin tone led to much animosity between slaves, as the group with lighter skin tones was bound to receive preferential treatment over the groups whose skin tone was darker. This caused division within people of African descent.

"Unfortunately, the effects of plantation politics with regards to intraracial division persist today. Intraracial discrimination among Blacks exists in two forms: colorism and borderism. Colorism or skin color prejudice is a prominent form of intraracial discrimination among Blacks that largely influences Black identity. Colorism is associated with notions of skin tone. [On the other hand,] the concept of borderism is associated with those who "cross the color line" by choosing not to align themselves with perceived Black behaviors or racial identity" (Busey, 2014).

"To treat intraracial racism and other matters of race as if they do not exist is a socially unjust practice as race makes up an integral part of our society. Both former president Barack Obama, in his speech at the 2004 National Democratic Convention, and former first lady Michelle Obama, in her 2013 commencement address at Boise State University, spoke about the derogatory nature in which some Blacks refer to their counterparts regarding their collegiate advancements, saying they are acting White" (Busey, 2014). Instead of being proud of each other for perhaps breaking a cycle of not attending college, we ridicule and marginalize one another. Marginalization is excluding others from mainstream lifestyle privileges.

Imagine a sheet of notebook paper. Along one side of the paper, there is a red line that separates the main portion of the page (the largest section) from the margin (the small section on the left side). Mainstream society would be equivalent to the right side (the large section), and marginalized people are those who are suppressed into the margin (the small section). Within the smaller section of the world, there are less opportunities and less privileges.

Is it not bad enough that Blacks as a race are already marginalized within American culture? Why would we subject ourselves to further marginalization within our own culture? We should strive to be more inclusive with one another rather than exclusive. The reality is it is predicated upon one's mindset.

Read the following excerpt from "Marginalization of African-Americans in the Social Sphere of Us Society" by Linde Riphagen.

African-Americans in the US have historically and continue to be consciously and unconsciously treated as others in US society, with all the resulting negative consequences. As adherents of critical race theory (CRT) have argued, this exclusion of an entire racial group has made it almost impossible for African Americans to deny sharing a common reality and therefore strive towards a much more communal outlook than is the case among white American individuals. It is argued that African-Americans have enabled the development and upwards mobility of white Americans and the former's marginalization continues to uplift society in periods of economic despair. However, this perception is threatening to white interests, and therefore attributes such as a faltering competitiveness in the economy and flagging interest in academic results are projected upon African-Americans to implicate them as themselves responsible for their dismal circumstances. The dominant norms set forth as the societal standard are defined by those in power and might therefore not apply to people of different cultures, backgrounds and races. 'Different' is in most cases interpreted as 'deviant' and sometimes as 'inferior.' Historically, white Americans were made to believe that African Americans were inferior, and although today it is less obviously presented as such, persists; that politicians have used African-Americans as scapegoats, that false images surrounding African-Americans have not been dispelled, continue to leave African-Americans outside mainstream society. It can clearly be seen that this perceived truth is perpetuated precisely because of its development and promotion by the white, dominant, mainstream spheres of society. Truth is what those in power portray it to be and what benefits the dominant group within a society, as in this case the white

Americans. The use of African-Americans for less desirable jobs and as a buffer in economic recession shows the continuous exploitation of African-Americans for the benefit of white US society. Therefore, an African-American is very well accepted as a clerk, but less so as a critic of the current status quo. The explanation is that the former is not very likely to question the US power structure, based on white interest, while the latter is. It can therefore be concluded that the clerk is more accepted as (s)he is more likely to stay within the boundaries of society in which white privilege can persist, while the critic ascends too far up the social ladder and might challenge the unjust practices and systems of society as a whole.

Historically, African-Americans can be seen as one of the racial groups at the ultimate bottom of the social ladder, this still having implications today in terms of persisting stigmatization, to the benefit of other more recently immigrated ethnic and racial groups. A lack of solidarity amongst different minority groups ensures the maintenance of white privileges. Furthermore, the continuous social stigmatization ensures that the white population will not strive together with minority groups for increased social justice by tackling the accumulation of wealth at the top of the socio-economic heap. The continuous stigmatization of African Americans ensures popular distraction from wealth inequalities as the rich get richer while companies cut employee benefits. This inequality has been historically created: the diversion of attention from wealthy landowners to the ever-to-blame slave is maintained even today.

(Riphagen, L. "Marginalization of African-Americans in the Social Sphere of Us Society" The Interdisciplinary Journal of International Studies Vol. 5. (2008) Reviewed December 9, 2020.)

Understanding how marginalization benefits mainstream America and continues to strengthen societal existing inequities, let's return to our discussion of intraracial discrimination. To demonstrate the reality of its existence within Black America, I will pinpoint poignant examples for intraracial discrimination that exists whether perpetuated from outside the race or within. My standpoint is this: Regardless of the origin or stimulus of intraracial discrimination, we as a race of people are the ones responsible to bring about a cessation of ill treatment amongst ourselves.

Read the following article abstract that provides a brief summation of black-on-black crime, a condition perpetuated by a combination of societal forces and intraracial discrimination:

> Although the Black community is not responsible for the external conditions that systematically create breeding grounds for crime, the community has the responsibility of doing what it can to attack the problem from within. This response is needed because such crime creates mistrust, uncertainty, fear, and anxiety in the community. More Blacks were killed by other Blacks in 1977 than died in the entire, 9-year Vietnam War. Such crime has driven businesses and jobs from the community. Property crimes alone have cost Blacks billions of dollars annually. Most importantly, the young have been profoundly affected by crime, as they are most often the perpetrators and the victims. Such underlying causes of crime as racism and oppression manifest themselves in high unemployment rates (the majority of first offenders are out of work), drug addiction, the breakdown of the urban family, and an unjust criminal justice system which shows more compassion for White victims of crime than for Black victims and which punishes Black criminals more severely than Whites. In addition, the prison system serves as a

training ground for further crime, and the media may contribute to the crime problem by portrayals of violence in movies and on television. Responses to the problem include the push for excellence program, community involvement programs, reformation of the criminal justice system to deal severely with criminals, development of a national plan for alleviating the economic ills of the ghetto, and the reaffirmation of religious values.

(Johnson, J. H. (editor). "Black on Black Crime - The Cause, The Consequences, The Cures" *Ebony* Vol. 34, Issue 10. (1978). Retrieved December 9, 2020.)

It is clear that the majority of the problems experienced by and within the Black community were initiated by outside forces. One major problem Black communities face is the infiltration of drugs into inner city neighborhoods, which has roots in the War on Drugs. Read the excerpt about President Richard Nixon, regarding the conspiracy to further debilitate Black Americans by flooding their communities with drugs, exacerbating drug usage and drug sales.

John Ehrlichman, Nixon's counsel and Assistant for Domestic Affairs, revealed in 1994, the real public enemy in 1971 wasn't really drugs or drug abuse. Rather the real enemies of the Nixon administration were the anti-war left and blacks, and the War on Drugs was designed as an evil, deceptive and sinister policy to wage a war on those two groups. In an article in the April 2016 issue of *The Atlantic* ("Legalize It All: How to win the war on drugs") author and reporter Dan Baum explains how "John Ehrlichman, the Watergate co-conspirator, unlocked for me one of the great mysteries of modern American history: How did the United States entangle itself in a policy of drug prohibition that has yielded so much misery and so few good results?" As Baum discovered, here's the dirty and disgusting secret to that great mystery of what must be the most expensive, shameful, and reprehensible failed government policy in US history.

Americans have been criminalizing psychoactive substances since San Francisco's anti-opium law of 1875, but it was Ehrlichman's boss, Richard Nixon, who declared the first "War on Drugs" in 1971 and set the country on the wildly punitive and counterproductive path it still pursues. I'd tracked Ehrlichman, who had been Nixon's domestic-policy adviser, to an engineering firm in Atlanta, where he was working on minority recruitment. At the time, I was writing a book about the politics of drug prohibition. I started to ask Ehrlichman a series of earnest, wonky questions that he impatiently waved away.

Baum stated: "You want to know what this was really all about?" he asked with the bluntness of a man who, after public disgrace and a stretch in federal prison, had little left to protect. "The Nixon campaign in 1968, and the Nixon White House after that, had two enemies: the antiwar left and black people. You understand what I'm saying? We knew we couldn't make it illegal to be either against the war or blacks, but by getting the public to associate the hippies with marijuana and blacks with heroin, and then criminalizing both heavily, we could disrupt those communities. We could arrest their leaders, raid their homes, break up their meetings, and vilify them night after night on the evening news. Did we know we were lying about the drugs? Of course, we did."

Nixon's invention of the War on Drugs as a political tool was cynical, but every president since — Democrat and Republican alike — has found it equally useful for one reason or another. Meanwhile, the growing cost of the Drug War is now impossible to ignore: billions of dollars wasted, bloodshed in Latin America and on the streets of our own cities, and millions of lives destroyed by draconian punishment that doesn't end at the prison gate; one of every eight black men has been disenfranchised because of a felony conviction.

(Perry, M. J. "The shocking story behind Richard Nixon's 'War on Drugs' that targeted blacks and anti-war activists." (2018). aei.org. Retrieved December 9, 2020.)

Let's examine drug sales and drug usage for a moment. From the passage we just read, as a conspiracy to further debilitate the Black community (as a whole), drugs were infiltrated into the community in an effort to entice those who were willing to be involved in sales as a means to better their personal finances, lifestyle, and overall well-being. Drugs sales, like any other business, is predicated on establishing a client base if one wants to do well. As with any other business owner who sales an actual product, one would not acquire the product to retain the product. The product is meant to be sold. So, the question becomes, "Who will be the client?"

Unless you are going to leave your realm of influence and your comfort zone and venture out into unknown territory, you will begin with people you know. That is the tactic used by most business owners, especially those who operate a "small business." Rarely, if ever, do people randomly go about and try to peddle their wares. If there is a venue that offers an opportunity in a community/public setting to sell, people may take the opportunity. Typically, people will make a start with friends and family.

Now, if your business is an illegitimate business, you most definitely will not venture into unknown territories attempting to peddle your wares because you don't know who the undercover police officers are and what areas are "safe" for illegal activity. So, where am I going with all of this? I'm getting to the conspiracy.

So, drugs were infiltrated into various Black communities, leading people to believe they could change their physical circumstances by selling an illegal product that if consumed could lead to a worsened physical condition, loss of mental capacities, sickness, or death. Without the full knowledge of the despair the drugs would bring upon a person, ill-informed people took the drugs and began to sell them to their own people because they had a dream of making it out of the situation they faced on a daily basis.

The downfalls that came with the illegal activity were/are numerous. First, many who consumed the illegal drugs became addicted. They developed a habit they could not afford financially, mentally, or emotionally. In many cases, their habit cost them their family, their friends, their job, their self-esteem, and their overall well-being. When a person is addicted, he/she is rendered unable to make good choices because all the body wants is for the addiction to be fed. Many families have been broken apart due to drug addiction. Children must exist with only one parent or no parent at all as the result of their parent(s)' drug addiction.

A second downfall of the drug conspiracy is the increased incarceration of Black individuals, mostly men, who are/were taken away from their families, the same families they are/were selling the drugs for in an attempt to get by or to get ahead. Once again, illegal drug sales contributed to the breakdown of the family.

Read the following report that details the disillusionment of drug sales and drug use and the portrayal of both in the media.

The bodies of people of color have a pernicious history of total exploitation and criminalization in the US. Like total war, total exploitation enlists and mobilizes the resources of mainstream society to obliterate the resources and infrastructure of the vulnerable. This has been done to Black people through a robust prison industrial complex that feeds on their vilification, incarceration, disenfranchisement, and erasure.

And the crack epidemic of the late 1980s and '90s is a clear example of this cycle.

Even though more white people reported using crack more than Black people in a 1991 National Institute on Drug Abuse survey, Black people were sentenced for crack offenses eight times more than whites. Meanwhile, there was a corresponding cocaine epidemic in white suburbs and college campuses that compelled the US to install harsher penalties for crack than for cocaine. For example, in 1986, before the enactment of federal mandatory minimum sentencing for crack cocaine offenses, the average federal drug sentence for African Americans was 11 percent higher than for whites. Four years later, the average federal drug sentence for African Americans was 49 percent higher.

Even through the '90s and beyond, the media and supposed liberal allies, like Hillary Clinton, designated Black children and teens as drug-dealing "super-predators" to mostly white audiences. The criminalization of people of color during the crack epidemic made mainstream white Americans comfortable knowing that this was a contained black-on-black problem.

It also left white America unprepared to deal with the approach of the opioid epidemic, which is often a white-on-white crime whose dealers will evade prison Unlike Black Americans who are sent to prison, these white dealers retain their right to vote, lobby, and hold on to their wealth.

(Machado, J. & Turner, K. "6 Myths About Black People in American." Feb. 18, 2020, www.vox.com/identities. Reviewed on Dec. 10, 2020.)

Notice how the inequities within our legal system tilted the balance in the favor of white citizens who were ingesting an equally dangerous and illegal substance but did not have their activities criminalized, while providing harsher treatments for

Blacks, causing a downward spiral within a downward spiral that is deeply imbedded and woven in the justice system.

A third impact of illegal drug sales is broken homes. When a parent is incarcerated due to illegal activities, he/she is taken away from a spouse who needs his/her support and from children who need his/her love, attention, and guidance. The same is true for drug users. When drug users become addicted, all normal practices, such as caring for offspring, become less important and the need to feed the addiction becomes the predominant concern. In both cases, parents are taken away from their families, leaving broken homes, unprotected and undernourished children, and stigmas.

At the same time, it is important to note broken homes had already greatly impacted the Black community, stemming from conditions that existed during the slave trade, such as husbands being purchased by one slave owner who may not have desired to purchase the wife as well. That left her to be transferred to another family with her children. This habitual tendency of slave owners leaving children with only one parent, normally the mother, caused the beginning of a long-standing tradition of broken homes. So, the existence of broken homes did not begin as a result of drug sales, but what was under reconstruction was placed in harm's way with neglect being part of the conspiracy package.

According to the Heather Williams, a history professor, "Some enslaved people lived in nuclear families with a mother, father, and children. In these cases, each family member belonged to the same owner. Others lived in near-nuclear families in which the father had a different owner than the mother and children. Both slaves and slaveowners referred to these relationships between men and women as 'abroad marriages.' A father might live several miles away on a distant plantation and walk, usually on Wednesday nights and Saturday evenings to see his family as his obligation to provide labor for an owner took precedence over his personal needs."

Furthermore, Williams noted, "Enslaved people lived with the perpetual possibility of separation through the sale of one or more family members. Slaveowners' wealth lay largely in the people they owned, therefore, they frequently sold and or purchased people as finances warranted. A multitude of scenarios brought about sale. An enslaved person could be sold as part of an estate when his owner died, or because the owner needed to liquidate assets to pay off debts, or because the owner thought the enslaved person was a troublemaker. A father might be sold away by his owner while the mother and children remained behind, or the mother and children might be sold. Enslaved families were also divided for inheritance when an owner died, or because the owners' adult children moved away to create new lives, taking some of the enslaved people with them. These decisions were, of course, beyond the control of the people whose lives they affected most. Sometimes an enslaved man or woman pleaded with an owner to purchase his or her spouse to avoid separation. The intervention was not always successful. Historian Michael Tadman has estimated that approximately one third of enslaved children in the upper South states of Maryland and Virginia experienced family separation in one of three possible scenarios: sale away from parents; sale with mother away from father; or sale of mother or father away from child. The fear of separation haunted adults who knew how likely it was to happen. Young children, innocently unaware of the possibilities, learned quickly of the pain that such separations could cost."
(Williams, Heather Andrea. "How Slavery Affected African American Families." Freedom's Story, TeacherServe©. National Humanities Center. Accessed on December 15, 2020. www.nationalhumanitiescenter.org.)

In all that was shared regarding illegal drug sales and use, the purpose was to drive the point home regarding snares that are set to entrap people, keeping them in a cycle of never being able to climb above. While pinpointing the sources of the snare, I am by no means excusing the choice or the behavior of those who participated in illegal activities. I am a firm believer of finding an alternate method to survive, even if it means putting in hard work and long hours. Finally, I digress with this- I am cognizant of the dichotomy of the juxtaposed sides, and I do understand how it must feel to be backed into a corner while feeling hopeless, trying to find a way out of a life of despair. Therefore, methods to end the cycle must frequently become infused in the conversation about change.

Another topic that warrants a discussion is the existence of gangs, prevailing gang activity, and the harm gang activity has caused innocent people. Before examining the harmful effects of gangs, let's discuss the reasons people continuously join gangs.

According to the research conducted by the Los Angeles Police Department, as a result of the prevalence of gangs in Los Angeles county and gang activity,

> [most youth] join a gang by either committing a crime or undergoing an initiation procedure wherein they are beaten ["jumped in"] by fellow gang members to test their courage and fighting ability. Their motivations for joining the gang are varied, but usually fall within one of the following categories:
> - Identity or Recognition - Being part of a gang allows the gang member to achieve a level of status he/she feels impossible outside the gang culture.
> - Protection - many members join because they live in the gang area and are, therefore, subject to violence by rival gangs. Joining guarantees support in case of attack and retaliation for transgressions.
> - Fellowship and Brotherhood - To the majority of gang members, the gang functions as an extension of the

family and may provide companionship lacking in the gang member's home environment. Many older brothers and relatives belong, or have belonged to the gang.

- Intimidation - Some members are forced to join if their membership will contribute to the gang's criminal activity. Some join to intimidate others in the community not involved in gang activity.
- Criminal Activity - Some join a gang to engage in narcotics activity and benefit from the group's profits and protection.

(LAPD Online. "Why Young People Join Gangs" www.lapdonline. Accessed December 16, 2020.)

Having an understanding of the reasons a person would join a gang does not neglect making an assessment of the outcomes of how a person's gang affiliation can impact the community in which the gang is situated. So, let's take a closer look at the specifics of two well-known gangs of the greater Los Angeles area: the Bloods and the Crips.

The Bloods gang was formed initially to compete against the influence of the Crips in Los Angeles. The rivalry originated in the 1960s when Raymond Washington and other Crips attacked Sylvester Scott and Benson Owens, two students at Centennial High School in Compton, California. As a result, Scott formed the Piru street-gang, the first "Bloods" gang. Owens subsequently established the West Piru gang. The Bloods was initially formed to provide members protection from the Crips. Many of the non-Crip gangs used to call one another "blood."

On March 21, 1972, shortly after a concert featuring Wilson Pickett and Curtis Mayfield, 20 youths belonging to the Crips attacked and robbed Robert Ballou Jr. outside the Hollywood Palladium. Ballou was beaten to death after refusing to give up his leather jacket. The sensational media coverage of the crime and the continued assaults by the Crips increased their notoriety. Several non-Crips gangs formed during this period were no match for the Crips and became concerned with the escalating Crip attacks. The Pirus, Black P. Stones, Athens Park Boys and other gangs not aligned with the Crips often clashed with them.

On June 5, 1972, three months after Ballou's murder, Fredrick "Lil Country" Garret was murdered by a Westside Crip. This marked the first Crips murder against another gang member and motivated non-Crip gangs to align with each other. The Brims struck back on August 4, 1972, by murdering Thomas Ellis, an original Westside Crip. By late 1972, the Pirus held a meeting in their neighborhood to discuss growing Crip pressure and intimidation. Several gangs that felt victimized by the Crips joined the Pirus to create a new federation of non-Crips neighborhoods. This alliance became the Bloods. The Pirus are therefore considered the founders of the Bloods.

By 1978, there were 15 Bloods sets. Crips still outnumbered Bloods 3 to 1. To assert their power, the Bloods became increasingly violent. During the 1980s, Bloods began distributing crack cocaine in Los Angeles. Blood membership soon rose dramatically as did the number of states in which they were present. These increases were primarily driven by profits from crack cocaine distribution. The huge profits allowed members to relocate to other cities and states.

(Harris, Donnie (2004). *Gangland*. Goose Creek, South Carolina: Holy Fire Publishing. p. 49. Reviewed December 16, 2020.)

(Alonso, Alex (2010). "Out of the Void". In Hunt, Darrell; Ramos, Ana-Cristina (eds.). *Black Los Angeles: American Dreams and Racial Realities*. New York City: NYU Press.)

Stanley Tookie Williams met Raymond Lee Washington in 1969, and the two decided to unite their local gang members from the west and east sides of South Central Los Angeles in order to battle neighboring street gangs. Most of the members were seventeen years old. Williams discounted the sometimes-cited founding date of 1969 in his memoir, *Blue Rage, Black Redemption*. Gang activity in South Central Los Angeles has its roots in a variety of factors dating to the 1950s, including post-World War II economic decline leading to joblessness and poverty, with racial segregation leading to the formation of black "street clubs" by young African American men who were excluded from organizations such as the Boy Scouts, and the waning of black nationalist organizations such as the Black Panther Party and the Black Power Movement.

By 1978, there were 45 Crips gangs, called sets, in Los Angeles. They were heavily involved in the production of PCP, marijuana and amphetamines. On March 11, 1979, Williams, a member of the Westside Crips, was arrested for four murders and on August 9, 1979, Washington was gunned down. Washington had been against Crip infighting and after his death several Crip sets started fighting against each other. The Crips' leadership was dismantled, prompting a deadly gang war between the Rollin' 60 Neighborhood Crips and Eight Tray Gangster Crips that led nearby Crip sets to choose sides and align themselves with either the Gangster Crips or Neighborhood Crips, waging all-out war in South Central and other cities. The East Coast Crips and the Hoover Crips directly severed their alliance after Washington's death.

By 1980, the Crips were in turmoil, warring with the Bloods and against each other. The gang's growth and power really took off in the early 1980s when crack cocaine hit the streets. Crips sets began distributing crack cocaine. The huge profits induced many Crips to establish new markets in other cities and states. As a result, Crip membership grew steadily and by the late 1980s it was one of the country's largest street gangs. In 1999, there were at least 600 Crips sets with more than 30,000 members transporting drugs in the United States.

(Williams, Stanley Tookie; Smiley, Tavis (2007). *Blue Rage, Black Redemption*. Simon & Schuster. pp. xvii–xix, 91–92, 136. Reviewed December 16, 2020.)
(Stacy Peralta (Director), Stacy Peralta & Sam George (writers), Baron Davis et al. (producer), Steve Luczo, Quincy "QD3" Jones III (executive producer) (2009). *Crips and Bloods: Made in America* (TV-Documentary). PBS Independent Lens series. Retrieved December 16, 2020.)
("Timeline: South Central Los Angeles". PBS (part of the "Crips and Bloods: Made in America" TV documentary). April 21, 2009. Retrieved December 16, 2020.)
(Sharkey, Betsy (2009-02-06). "Review: 'Crips and Bloods: Made in America'." *Los Angeles Times*. Retrieved December 16, 2020.)
(Cle Sloan (Director), Antoine Fuqua and Cle Sloan (producer), Jack Gulick (executive producer) (2009). Keith Salmon (ed.). *Bastards of the Party* (TV-Documentary). HBO. Retrieved December 16, 2020.)
(Harris, Donnie (October 2004). *Gangland*. Reviewed December 16, 2020.)
(Hunt, Darnell; Ramon, Ana-Christina (May 2010). *Black Los Angeles*. Reviewed December 16, 2020.)

Drive-by shootings is another problem that often occurs in inner cities and are usually associated with gang activity. Kelly Dedel, a criminal researcher, discovered the following when she conducted research on drive-by shootings:

A drive-by shooting refers to an incident when someone fires a gun from a vehicle at another vehicle, a person, a structure, or another stationary object. Drive-by shootings are a subset of more general gun violence and are less common than incidents in which someone approaches another on foot and fires at him or her. Many drive-by shootings involve multiple suspects and multiple victims. Using a vehicle allows the shooter to approach the intended target without being noticed and then to speed away before anyone reacts. The vehicle also offers some protection in the case of return fire. In some situations, drive-by shootings are gang-related; in others, they are the result of road rage or personal disputes between neighbors, acquaintances, or strangers and are not related to gang membership. Non-gang-related drive-by shootings are not well researched, but journalistic accounts and police reports suggest that these constitute a significant proportion of the drive-by shootings to which police respond. Because of their prevalence, they are included in this guide, despite the dearth of research about their motivations and the lack of evaluative research showing which responses are most effective with this type of drive-by shooting. Even if a drive-by shooting problem is not patently gang-related, some of what is known about gang-related shootings may inform responses to other kinds of drive-by shootings.

Gun violence perpetrated by other means is far more prevalent than gun violence facilitated by vehicle use. For example, in West Oakland, Calif., offenders were 10 times more likely to walk up to the intended victim and shoot him or her than to use a vehicle to facilitate the attack (Wilson & Riley 2004). Similarly, an analysis of San Diego homicides from 1999 through 2003 revealed that drive-by shootings accounted for about 10 percent of all of them (Wilson et al 2004).

Although some drive-by shootings result in the victim's death, many result in nonfatal injuries to the intended victim or innocent bystanders. Whether the shooting is lethal depends less on the intent of the offender and more on the location of the wound and the speed of medical attention. The intended targets may be slow to mobilize in the face of an unanticipated attack, and their reactions may be delayed by drugs or alcohol. The specifics of a drive-by shooting—in which the shooter is aiming a gun out the window of a moving vehicle at a moving target, and is often inexperienced in handling a gun—mean that shots often go wild and injure people or damage property that was not the intended target. Deaths of innocent bystanders often receive significant media attention and result in passionate public outcry, particularly when the victim is extremely young, has a debilitating medical condition, or was shot while inside a supposedly "safe" structure, such as their home or place of worship.

For example, in Los Angeles, of over 2,000 victims of drive-by shootings in 1991, only 5 percent were fatally injured. Over half sustained a gunshot wound to the leg (Hutson, Anglin, & Eckstein 1996; Hutson, Anglin, & Pratts 1994).

One study of Los Angeles drive-by shootings in the early 1990s found that the proportion of those injured in drive-by shootings who were innocent bystanders ranged between 38 to 59 percent each year (Hutson, Anglin, & Eckstein 1996).

(Dedel, K. (2007). "The Problem with Drive-By Shootings." Problem-Oriented Guides for Police, Problem-Specific Guide No. 47. Washington, D.C.: U.S. Department of Justice, Office of Community Oriented Policing Services.)

As noted in our surveyance of intraracial discrimination inherent in the continuing existence of "color codes," the effects of marginalization, the impacts of the infiltration of drugs, and gang formation and involvement, Black communities must reassess the way in which we communicate and interact with one another. Why? Because breaking the negative cycles is our responsibility. It is incumbent upon us to effectuate change in our everyday practices. We cannot sit idly by and wait for outside entities to come and repair that which we have had and continue to have a hand in causing destruction.

As a reminder, I began this chapter with Hosea 4:6, *"My people are destroyed for the lack of knowledge...."* With this verse, we are directed to obtain knowledge. Then, we must take account of the part we play in tearing down our own communities. Next, we must undertake the responsibility of breaking the cycle of internal destruction and learn ways to mend. Mending will lead to advancement in attaining wealth across the board: finances, interpersonal relationships, family structure, health concerns, and in developing relations with other races.

One way to break the cycle of internal destruction is changing people's perception with use of media influence. And this has actually already begun as it relates to preferring one tone of skin over others. Unlike two decades ago, we now see people of all races, sizes, and complexions in commercials, television shows, and movies. Their appearances are hardly equal across all genres or on all television channels, but great strides have been made. How did this change occur? Those who have aspirations for the arts continued to show up at auditions, displaying their talents until their gifts could no longer be denied or ignored- regardless of the color of their skin.

Another way to alleviate Black-on-Black terror and animosity is to call a moratorium on all negative behavior. This notion is not a novel idea. It was executed between the Bloods and the Crips.

In April of 1992, Crips and Bloods in the Watts neighborhood in southern Los Angeles convened to negotiate peace. The Grape Street Crips from the Jordan Downs Projects, the P Jay Watts Crips from the Imperial Courts housing projects, the Bounty Hunter Bloods from the Nickerson Gardens housing projects, and the Hacienda Village Bloods agreed to a ceasefire agreement following the death of Henry Pico, who had been shot execution-style by LAPD officers during a blackout in the Imperial Courts housing project. On April 28, 1992, representatives from these four gangs signed a formal peace treaty at a masjid in Watts. The treaty was modeled on the 1949 Armistice Agreements reached between Israel and Egypt. Within days of the truce, despite the relative lawlessness caused by the 1992 Los Angeles riots, most of the African-American gangs in the city declared themselves at peace and there were no major flare-ups in violence. The Watts truce is generally credited with contributing to the trend in declining street violence rates in Los Angeles.

(Stoltze, Frank (April 28, 2012). "Forget the LA Riots – historic 1992 Watts gang truce was the big news". *89.3 KPCC Southern California Public Radio.* Retrieved December 16, 2020.)

In April 2017, D. Amari Jackson reported the following: "Along with other gang intervention experts, former members, activists and local residents, Aqeela Sherrills will commemorate the 25th anniversary of the truce this week with a series of discussions, films and intervention events."

(Jackson, D. A. (2017). "The Lasting Legacy of the 1992 Watts Gang Truce." www.atlantablackstar.com. Reviewed December 16, 2020.)

A twenty-five-year truce is worthy of celebration because with the truce came elevated levels of peace and safety for the inhabitants of the communities in which the gangs operate.

Another method to overcome intraracial tension is to provide more opportunities in education. As mentioned earlier, tension can stem from the educational variances that exist between individuals. Thus, providing additional educational resources in underserved communities will give more students an opportunity to excel scholastically. Equal educational opportunities will lead to more high school graduates, more college attendance, and more college degrees, leading to higher paying jobs.

Although I only presented a few ways to eradicate intraracial discrimination, the possibilities are numerous. Regardless of which method a person deems viable for bringing about positive change, there is one component we must all strive to remember:

Do not fall victim to the divisive plans America began concocting against Black Americans centuries ago. Doing so will only elongate our time in this cycle, and eventually, tear down centuries of blood, sweat, and tears expended by our forerunners.

Chapter Five

The Transference of Wealth

Approximately three ago, the Lord began speaking to me about a wealth transfer that He can and will manifest in the earth realm. His words rang so heavily in my spirit that I began to include a small portion of what the Lord told me each time I preached (regardless of the main subject of the sermon), alerting my audiences to prepare for a mighty move of God. Informing people to prepare for a mighty move of God is not something Christians never hear or hear infrequently. They hear the same general prophecy time and time again, and while they desire to believe the word of the minister or prophet who delivers it, it begins to sound similar to a broken record. Those words- mighty move of God- have become commonplace in Christendom because of who God is. We always expect great movements by the omni-potent God.

So, when I shared the "magical" repetitive words, I attempted to be more specific about what God desires to do on our behalf rather than speaking in generalities. However, it was a little difficult to do because God never shared with me the how, when, or why. He just kept reminding me of Proverbs 13:22, which says, *"A good man leaveth an inheritance to his children's children: and the wealth of the sinner is laid up for the just,"* with the emphasis on the latter portion of the verse. That verse alone speaks volumes to me, telling me that God is going to provide for His own in a monumental manner, regardless of how the situation may presently reveal itself.

Outside of the pulpit, I shared the prophetic word with my co-laborers in the gospel with whom I have a personal relationship. Upon hearing the prophecy, they readily agreed with me about the wealth transfer, believing that the time for a change of present-day economic imbalances between the races had come and would soon be realized. Some even said they too believed such a move of God was on the horizon and felt in their spirit the wealth transfer was imminent.

What was most poignant to me was the weight of the prophecy on my shoulders and in my belly. Even if I had really wanted to, I could not shake the words of the Lord loose from me. I wholeheartedly believed what the Lord had shared with me was not only for myself but for others as well and that what He had planned would correct a wrong that was a direct result of generations and generations of wealth imbalance. The weight I carried compelled me to share the prophecy as often as I could.

As time moved on and years passed, I watched for signs regarding God's promise. There were specific things that happened in my life that showed me God was moving. For instance, in 2017, I was blessed to sign a contract agreeing to receive payment of $5,000 per class I taught, and the classes were only three days long and were to be taught from Tuesday to

Thursday during a given week. Teaching two to three classes per month caused an increase in my take-home pay by $10,000 to $15,000 per month. Let me reiterate- that was over and above my regular pay for the classes I teach each semester at the colleges. The contract extended well into 2018, adding $85,000 to my annual salary.

With God's grace and favor being poured into my life, I believed the prophecy could be coming to pass. At the same time, I did not believe the contract was what the Lord had spoken to me about. That was simply a drop in the bucket of what God was planning. In other words, it was a precursor to the "real deal." God was only giving me a sample of what He was planning. Moreover, the contract was sent as a reminder of what the Lord had shared with me.

I must admit that as time passed, there were times when the prophecy was heavy in my spirit, but never as heavy as it was when He first told me. All in all, I still trusted God because I know Him to be true to His word. Furthermore, the Lord Himself told me about the changes He would effectuate. He did not send a prophet to tell me His plans, leaving me with the option to believe or not believe. He told me Himself, leaving me no choice at all of whether I would believe His words. Then, my assignment was to share the prophecy with others.

Now that I am sharing the prophecy with you via this book, it is up to you whether or not you will receive it in your heart and into your spirit to prepare for the coming shift that will take place in the earth realm. The choice is yours.

Another time the words of the Lord came back to me, flooding my spirit with excitement, was on Friday, May 1, 2020, in the midst of the COVID-19 (the novel coronavirus) world-wide pandemic. That afternoon, the Lord reminded me of the same prophetic word He had given me several years prior. However, when He brought the prophecy back to my remembrance, He added a bit more. That time, the Lord told me, "If you ask, they will do it." Mentally, I translated those words to, "Ask, and your request will be granted." Matthew 7:7 says, *"Ask, and it will be given to you; seek, and you will find; knock, and it will be opened to you."* So, in essence, the Lord was reminding me of His Holy Word.

Let me digress for a moment to fill in the details that occurred prior to May 1, 2020. Two months earlier, in March 2020, a stay-at-home order was in effect in California, due to the worldwide outbreak of COVID-19. The stay-at-home order caused most people to stay home from work, go to school from home (or temporarily have no school at all) or to close their small business. Restaurants closed, freeways were empty, and the store shelves were nearly bare.

When the pandemic hit, taking our nation by storm with layoffs, furloughs, and soaring unemployment rates, the world was literally in pandemonium. Not only that but people were contracting the virus, causing emergency rooms to be filled to capacity. Then, the death toll began, with the numbers increasing daily. Families were devastated; communities were financially impacted.

In the midst of all the overwhelming shock of how the world and specifically our country could be turned upside down in what felt like overnight, the Lord began to move through the Treasury Department of the United States government in the form of a stimulus package to provide Americans what they needed to care for themselves and their families.

The stimulus package, aptly named the Coronavirus Aid, Relief, and Economic Security (C.A.R.E.S.) Act was the largest stimulus package in the history of the United States, totaling a resounding $2.2 billion, designed to stimulate the American economy to keep it from crashing. Acts 10:34-35, *"Then Peter began to speak: 'I now realize how true it is that God does not show favoritism but accepts from every nation the one who fears him and does what is right'"* immediately jumped into my spirit reminding me that like God, the government had to be impartial while in the midst of a national crisis.

That was the one time when every nation, every land, every race, and every socioeconomic status was impacted by the same thing at the same time to the degree nations were suffering. Given those circumstances and the urgency associated with the deadly virus, the government did not have time to render their normal tactics of scrutiny to find grey areas that could be used to deny a person benefits or funding.

As part of the stimulus package, the Small Business Association publicized two specific loan programs (amongst a host of others) for which business owners could qualify. One of the programs was the Economic Injury Disaster Loan (EIDL). As soon as the word spread that funds to assist struggling business were available, the website was flooded with applicants. The applications were completed by many, while others struggled to understand what was being asked of them. Then, documents had to be uploaded to support the information on the application.

In an effort to obtain funds for one of my small businesses, I went onto the website and went through the cumbersome steps. It took days to gather the documents and attempt to submit them. In the end, I was unsuccessful and never heard anything from the SBA.

Meanwhile, news about the Payroll Protection Program (PPP) began to flood the airwaves and travel by word of mouth. I decided to look into the benefits of the program. The foremost benefit was the loan would be used to keep people employed, allowing them to pay their personal expenses and keep food in the refrigerator. Additionally, the loan could be forgiven. I applied for the loan and received a response two days later. In the email, I was prompted to go into a portal, where I would be asked to submit documentation for my business. When I attempted to access the portal, the link was inoperable. I tried again a few days later, but my efforts were to no avail.

Meanwhile, I was completing the PPP application for an organization I belong to, attempting to gain much-needed funds. There were some bumps along the way, but I could see the end of the process getting closer. Seeing success on the horizon, I remembered my own efforts regarding my personal business loan. A week had passed, and I had not considered trying the link again. I was actually beginning to believe that trying to complete the application was a lost cause.

One night before going to bed, I decided I would call the lender the next morning to share my concerns about the inoperable portal link, hoping there was an alternative method to submitting the documents. The next day, which was Friday, May 1, 2020. I went back to the email that contained the portal link to search for the correct number to call. In my spirit, I felt an unction to attempt the link again. To my delight, it worked.

I quickly submitted the requested documents and breathed a sigh of relief. Meanwhile, I continued climbing over the hurdles the organization's application presented. Not an hour after submitting the required supporting documents for my loan application, I received an email from someone at the lender's company. I clicked on the email, and inside was a link to a promissory note for the PPP loan. In disbelief and while holding my breath, I electronically signed the documents. I didn't understand what was occurring, and I refused to allow myself to get excited about the loan being be funded (although I had signed the loan documents), so I said nothing to anyone.

I continued working on the documents for the organization, attempting to at least get the application to the status mine had reached, even while not knowing what the final outcome would be. After successfully submitting the documents for the organi-zation, I decided to shift gears and run errands. In the midst of submitting the documents for the two applications, I had received an email from one of my clients who wanted to have his second book published. The email notified me of his impending deposit into my bank account for his book.

While I was running errands, I checked my bank account to see if my client had been true to his word and made his deposit. If so, I would send him a receipt once I returned to my office. When I checked my account, I nearly passed out from sheer surprise. Instead of seeing a deposit from my client, a deposit from the SBA was sitting in my account. When I finally began to breathe again, I was able to share the news with my husband, sons, and close friends.

Later that day, while I was talking to a close friend of mine, it was then that the Lord spoke to me telling me all we had to do was ask. I immediately understood that asking, in the sense of the SBA loan programs, was completing and submitting the applications. The application, in essence, was a petition that was being submitted.

When the Lord spoke, once again His words resonated in my spirit. It wasn't because He was preparing me for what He was going to do. Instead, He was telling me that the transfer had begun in a major way. The Lord was apprising me of exactly what He *was* doing at that very moment. He was filling the needs of people, and He was moving expeditiously. So, I immediately began spreading the word about the SBA loan programs.

Over the next several months, many businesses throughout the country applied for funding and were approved. The program initially closed on June 30, although it did reopen less than a week later when President Trump signed it back into effect. However, at that point, many of the lenders who were involved in taking applications and disseminating loans did not reopen their doors or online loan portals. So, the opportunities for funding had decreased.

Take a look at the charts on the next page, which were obtained directly from the Small Business Association's website. You will find an overview of the number of loans disbursed and the amount of money associated with the Payroll Protection Program.

Summary of PPP Approved Lending
(thru June 30, 2020)

Loan Count	Net Dollars	Lender Count
4,885,388	$521,483,817,756	5,461

Lender Size	Lender Count	Loan Count	Net Dollars	% of Amt
>$50 B in Assets	34	1,639,892	$189,773,791,634	36%
$10 B to $50 B in Assets	89	739,912	$100,724,547,553	19%
<10 B in Assets	5,338	2,505,584	$230,985,478,569	44%

Loan Size Distribution

Loan Size	Loan Count	Net Dollars	% of Count	% of Amount
$50K and Under	3,262,529	$58,652,110,621	66.80%	11.20%
>$50K - $100K	673,563	$47,963,195,310	13.80%	9.20%
>$100K - $150K	291,019	$35,626,300,937	6.00%	6.80%
>$150K - $350K	376,113	$84,452,629,388	7.70%	16.20%
>$350K - $1M	199,456	$113,442,814,223	4.10%	21.80%
>$1M - $2M	53,030	$73,522,278,271	1.10%	14.10%
>$2M - $5M	24,838	$73,841,502,099	0.50%	14.20%
>$5M	4,840	$33,982,986,907	0.10%	6.50%

Overall average loan size is approximately $107,000.
86.5% of all loans were for less than $150,000.

Three months after I had attempted the cumbersome EIDL application and after a hoard of complaints were presented to the SBA from business owners, regarding the difficulties involved with applying for much needed revenue, the seven-page EIDL appli-cation was removed from the website. The program was temporarily closed, and eventually the extensive application was replaced with a streamlined, more user-friendly application. The news regarding the new application and the reopening of the program went viral on June 15, 2020. Personally, I received an email on Tuesday, June 16, from a tax firm I had visited earlier in the year. I wasn't sure how the process would go the second time around, but I decided it was worth an attempt.

Immediately after receiving the email, I clicked on the link that took me directly to the application. I commenced to filling it out, doing so in about ten minutes. After filling out the application, I received an application number. Two days later, I received the grant portion of the funding, and on the third day, I received full funding for my loan. Just as one month and a half before, I was in awe regarding the ease of the process, and the Lord kept assuring me it was only the tip of the iceberg.

After receiving funding from both the PPP and EIDL programs, I was really fired up about what God was doing in my life, and I believed that because He is no respecter of persons what He made happen for me, He would make happen for others. So, I began calling other people, starting with my own family members who own a business to ask if they had heard about the programs, specifically the EIDL program because it literally required no paperwork submission.

From there, I began assisting some people with their applications in an effort to keep their small businesses afloat during a time when most businesses had been ordered by their state to close, leaving them with virtually no income. People were hurting and were without a clue about how they would navigate financially through the pandemic.

In all my efforts and compassion for my fellow man, I assisted with loans from June until the program closed on August 31. Not everyone qualified for the loan, but most people whom I assisted did qualify and had their loans funded. The loans I assisted with released approximately $1,000,000 into the hands of business owners, who were all Black Americans. When the applicants shared with me the news of their approved applications and that the money had been deposited into their bank account, I celebrated with them. And, after giving them many words of advice regarding keeping good financial records, I prayed over their business and told them to keep their eyes and ears open for the next move of God.

Part of my words of advice included a discussion regarding misappropriating funds. The Lord had made it very clear when He shared the prophecy with me, revealing to me through the plight of the Israelites, their exodus from Egypt, and their time in the wilderness, that we should be careful to use the funds dispensed in the purposes for which they were intended. In showing me what parts of their plight on which to focus, the Lord showed me what happened to the gold the Israelites were instructed to ask for and subsequently received.

In the midst of the wilderness, while Moses was on Mount Sinai meeting with God, while He wrote the Ten Commandments upon tablets of stone with His finger, the Israelites convinced Aaron to create an entity for them to worship. Aaron asked for their gold earrings and subsequently fashioned a golden calf for which the Israelites could worship. Was the creation of a golden calf the purpose the Lord provided the wealth to the Israelites? No, of course not. When we use funds the Lord provided to us for purposes other than which they were intended, we are guilty of misappropriating funds. Doing this will require us to answer to God directly.

Reviewing all that had occurred in a few months' time, I knew what was occurring in the lives of so many business owners, as well as my own life, was abnormal because under "normal" operating procedures, it would be difficult for people of color with low to moderate financial resources to obtain funding from the government or banking institutions for business capital. But the Lord was speaking loudly and clearly, telling me that this was an opportunity for everyone across the board to *apply* for various business funds that had been released in billions upon billions of dollars.

Unfortunately, not all businesses were successful in obtaining funds, and yes, an exorbitant amount of money went to business that were not currently demonstrating need rather than businesses that were folding before the very consciousness of America. However, on a more upbeat note, millions of businesses that were previously underfunded were successful in receiving funds. That alone enabled millions of small businesses to stay open, keep bills paid, place food on the table, and retain their employees.

What is even more awesome is many new entrepreneurs sprang up and started long-desired businesses they may not have been able to begin. Although there was/is much devastation surrounding the ever-increasing number of COVID-19 cases and the still rising death toll, there was/is a silver lining that appeared in the midst of the novel coronavirus pandemic. God demonstrated to me that He could move in *any* situation. He is yet in control of the universe, and He has not ceased to perform miracles.

But, if I had any doubt that it was God who was moving, about a month later, in July 2020, I received another confirmation. Late one night (in the midnight hour), as I was sitting on my bed, I was wide awake thinking about all God had done. I should have been asleep, but I was pondering a million plus ideas. In the still of the night, Holy Spirit told me to apply for another EIDL loan for another business I have. It had not entered my mind or my heart to apply for that particular business, and I won't into detail why not. Just know that it was not my own idea, greed, or trying to 'come up' that I did what Holy Spirit said to do. I acted in obedience.

A few mornings later, I was awake at 4am. I walked into the living room and sat in a recliner and began praying. In the midst of praying, a text message came in- yes, at 4am. The text was from one of my banks, notifying me a deposit had come in. That was odd to me. When I read the text and saw the amount, I knew it was the money from the loan being deposited. At the moment, the Lord said, "I have not forgotten you." A single tear ran down my face and a sigh escaped my lips, as I realized I could move forward with the dream of a lifetime.

But, that's not it! A few weeks after that Malachi 3:10, *"Bring ye all the tithes into the storehouse, that there may be meat in mine house, and prove me now herewith, saith the LORD of hosts, if I will not open you the windows of heaven, and pour you out a blessing, that there shall not be room enough to receive it,"* jumped into my spirit. I almost dared not to present another petition before the Lord, but believing His Word led me to make a request. I thanked God profusely for all He had already done; then, I reminded Him of His Word, knowing it applies to me as I am an avid tithe giver along with giving offerings.

In all sincerity, I told the Lord, "I thank you Father for the blessings you have poured out to me, but I still have room to receive. Your Word says, you will pour me out a blessing that I would _not_ have room to receive it. Lord, pour out the overflow." (These are close to my exact words as I remember.) In August

2020, the Lord blessed me with the overflow, and when I saw the money in my account, tears ran down my face.

Many business owners were blessed by the EIDL program, just as many were by the PPP program. Also, the EIDL program had an imbedded benefit for those who did not qualify for the loan. They were able to still receive assistance by way of a grant during that unprecedented time. Read the following excerpt from a press release issued by the Small Business Administration that was released on July 11, 2020.

> Today, the U.S. Small Business Administration announced the conclusion and success of the Economic Injury Disaster Loan (EIDL) Advance program, which provided U.S. small businesses, non-profits and agricultural businesses a total of $20 billion in emergency funding. In order to assist the greatest number of small businesses, the EIDL Advance provided $1,000 per employee up to a maximum of $10,000. Recipients did not have to be approved for a loan to receive the Advance, and the Advance provided an interim but vital source of funds while applicants awaited a decision on their loan application.
>
> *"Following the enactment of COVID-19 emergency legislation, the SBA provided nearly six million small businesses employing 30.5 million people with $20 billion through the unprecedented EIDL Advance program," Administrator Jovita Carranza said. "This program, built from the ground up in less than two weeks, assisted millions of small businesses, including non-profit organizations, sole proprietors and independent contractors, from a wide array of industries and business sectors."*

I stated earlier both programs closed around the end of summer and fall of 2020. However, as I was writing this book during December 2020, Congress had just approved a $900 billion stimulus package that reinstated both SBA loan programs. With that wonderful news that our country has been anxiously awaiting, it is my prayer that business owners who were previously unaware of the business loan opportunities would somehow come to learn about them, complete the applications, and receive the much-needed funding. Funding will be a continuation of what God is doing to level the financial playing field.

As I mentioned earlier in this chapter, there is a silver lining to COVID-19. Listed below is consequential evidence of the prophecy being manifested during this season:

- Many people became debt free during COVID-19. While many Americans suffered from lay-offs and furloughs from their primary, and in most cases only, source of income, others received unexpected benefits as a result of the coronavirus. The unexpected benefits led to an influx of cash, allowing individuals and families an opportunity to clear past due bills. Not only did many people bring accounts current, others were able to close accounts by paying them in full. Furthermore, many credit companies were willing to forgive debt or at least offer a settlement to close an account. Most companies understood the hardship families were facing and realized it would do no one any good to hold the families hostage with the past due amounts during such a national crisis. It was better to take the money they were able to receive and wipe the slate clean.
- Many businesses were spared from experiencing permanent closure by migrating their business services/products online. Because of the level of technology that is currently available to the everyday consumer and business owner, some businesses were easily migrated to online

platforms to continue offering business services and products to faithful customers. And businesses that were able to personally deliver the products to their clients held an additional foothold of stability from suffering closure.

- New businesses began while people were furloughed from their "regular" jobs. With people being laid off or permanently released from their jobs, many had at least eight hours per day of free time on their hands. With no professional responsibilities required of them, they were free to explore other ways to procure finances. Many began home-based businesses, such as food services (ranging from baked goods to full meals), craft businesses, t-shirt businesses, to mobile car detailing. Without the existence of the pandemic, many people would still be working a job that was unfulfilling, but they began operating a business that demonstrates their heart's desires.

- Unemployment supplemental benefits provided additional monies each week for furloughed workers, released workers, and business owners. Unemployment benefits were expanded to employees and business owners who under normal circumstances would not qualify. In an effort to having as many people comply with stay-at-home orders, employees across the board were offered unemployment benefits. Over the course of a few months, the federal government realized the weekly amounts people were qualifying for was insufficient to sustain their livelihood. As a result, as part of the C.A.R.E.S. Act, additional funds were poured into the state-level unemployment fund. These additional funds, in amounts ranging from $300 to $600 a week, enabled individuals to fall into one of the first three categories mentioned above.

Meanwhile, even with the blessings that are flowing through governmental programs, there is still much work to do to see a widespread existence of wealth and better opportunities in Black communities. What can we do (individually and collectively) to assist ourselves and others in growing wealth and turning a corner while continuing to exist in the midst of an affluent society but not yet reaping the benefits?

1. Support Black Businesses
    As a community of people, there are many thriving Black businesses, ranging from hair and barber salons to legal services. However, there is a lack of support of Black-owned businesses, especially within the Black community. Instead of supporting Black-owned businesses, our dollars are spent elsewhere. We definitely immerse our capital into city malls, neighborhood grocery outlets, and online shopping.
    If we stop and survey what other cultures are doing to break through the financial ceiling, we will realize they set up public venues to sell their products, making themselves visible. We will also notice their counterparts supporting them, by purchasing what they have to offer. They strive to keep their dollars within their communities. This has been witnessed in Hispanic/Mexican communities as well as Asian communities. In order to support more Black businesses, we need to know they exist. One way to publicize Black-owned businesses is to join/create an online registry and by joining the local Black Chamber of Commerce, and by using social media outlets, such as Instagram.

2. Giving A Hand Up
    Those who have climbed the educational and economic ladders can give a hand up to others, showing them how they can achieve their personal goals, dreams, and desires by taking

advantage of available opportunities. While there are many public notices regarding what can be done to achieve one's goals, there is oftentimes little information on *how* to achieve the goal. Many people are intimidated about asking questions and speaking to others outside of their race. Therefore, it is imperative for us to avail ourselves to talk to those who need information, giving them an opportunity to ask questions.

While giving a hand up, we must make ourselves relatable to others; otherwise, we are just another road block in their path. To make ourselves available, we can reach out to churches, schools of all grade levels, community centers, and group homes. However, the most effective way to train the next generation is to begin teaching at home. When one person in a family possesses knowledge, he/she has a familial responsibility to teach others in the family.

Note: Giving a hand up does not necessarily refer to those within the specific community in which you were raised. It simply means lending a hand to anyone who can use your knowledge or expertise wherever you may be.

3. Business Training and Economic Development
    For promising future entrepreneurs, as well as those already in the throes of their business development, ongoing business training should be offered. Of course, business owners should probably take a business course or two at the local community college to learn business basics; however, someone with business expertise and acumen could take a semester-long course and streamline it into a weekend course, giving the nuts and bolts to future and current business owners.
    Courses of this nature could take business owners further into being and becoming successful in their business endeavors. Furthermore, it can prevent them from falling into pitfalls along the way, especially those that may prove expensive and

cause the business to fold before it gains foundational strength.

4. Maximize Spending Power

Many people face a monthly challenge: having more month than money. That means, before the month is over, the money is gone, creating an end-of-the-month strain or worry and distress each and every month. One way to overcome this ongoing challenge is to create a budget. A budget can be used to reduce and eventually eliminate the end-of-the-month crisis many people face.

To begin, you need to make a list of all expenses. Begin with survival expenses- items that are necessary for survival, such as mortgage/rent, car payment, utilities, insurances (health, life, car, home owners), and food. If you drive to work, include gas as an expense. For those who are tithers, be sure to include tithing in your budget. After all necessary items for survival have been included in the budget, other expenses, such as credit cards and personal loans, can be added to the list.

Notice: Budgeting for "habits" is not included here, as they are not necessary for survival. Once the budget is created, discipline is required to stick to the budget. Without having discipline to execute the budget, you will return to the "status quo" of having the end-of-the-month strain.

Even for those of you who have a sufficient amount of funds to pay all your monthly expenses and have quite a bit of money left over, budgeting will assist in spending less on frivolous items.

5. Changing Spending Habits

Now that you have considered creating a budget, let's consider spending habits. Ask yourself this question, "Do I have the 'Treat Myself' syndrome?" The "Treat Myself" syndrome is when you feel the need to treat yourself every time you get paid. First of all, there is nothing wrong with treating yourself. You work hard for your money, and you should be the first one to enjoy the benefits of your labor. However, if you get paid every week or every two weeks, you are giving yourself a lot of treats, and financially that can impact your monthly budget. Consider treating yourself once a month or once a quarter.

The next question you should ask yourself is, "Do I engage in valueless spending?" That refers to spending money on items that have no intrinsic or extrinsic value. Similar to treating yourself every payday, valueless spending can be habitual, leading one onto a path of having more month than money.

Aside from creating a budget, you may want to create a list of additional spending you engage in, just so you can see where your money is actually going. You may really be surprised with the amount of money you release spontaneously each month. Viewing the list can assist in curtailing valueless spending.

6. Have a Savings Plan

Many would say creating a savings plan is part of creating a monthly budget. I am going to approach this subject another way. It is easy to tell someone to save money each month when the person speaking has managed to do so. However, I realize that for some, there is absolutely no money left to save and if a person did take money from the incoming funds to place into a savings account, he/she would eventually be required to withdraw the money out of savings to fulfill a financial obligation, making the whole point of saving moot. So, let's approach this from a different vantage point.

A few months after you have created your monthly budget and curtailed your extraneous spending habits, consider creating a savings account. If you find it feasible to do so, ask yourself what amount can you comfortably deposit into a savings account. When you figure out what that amount is, start saving. Keep in mind that savings are meant to be saved over a long period of time. Also, savings can be used for different reasons. The main reason people save is for emergencies, such as unexpected car or home repairs, an illness that prevents one from working, etc. Savings could also be for a child's college fund or to make a major purpose, such as a vehicle, a down payment on a home, an extravagant dream vacation, etc.

There are many reasons people save. Once you begin your savings, try hard to stick to your plan, as you will see the benefits of saving, even if it takes some time.

7. Invest

Now, let's talk about increasing your financial worth. Taking a portion of your monthly income can also be used to invest to grow your resources and your available capital and to increase your financial portfolio. Talking to an investment banker who can provide you with methods to get started will be a beneficial first step.

In rebuilding, restructuring, and revitalizing the Black community, in an effort to work against the forces that have caused division and against the ill works we have manifested within ourselves, we can turn circumstances around for all of us who are willing and able. We want to rise above the depths of prejudice and systemic racism that are tantamount in our nation, seeing a more prosperous tomorrow than we are currently experiencing today. Inherent in all of the restorative methods that are listed above are the following: changing learned behaviors we were taught during our youth, teaching the youth of today healthy ways to exist and engage with finances, and creating wealth by bettering ourselves and supporting one another. Most of all, we must not forget that God has not forgotten us! With all of these factors in place, then and only then, can we change our existence and lay a stronger foundation full of love, trust, communication, and hope for a promising future.

Sharing the various methods that can be used to restore, uplift, and encourage a forward-moving community of people in no way discounts or discredits the movements that have already been initiated over the last several hundreds of years. Due to the enormity of the task we are faced with, we must press onward, while being dedicated to becoming and remaining change makers, until we achieve the results we so desire. So, while we give credit to whom credit is due, we cannot rest until all efforts have been fully realized.

Chapter Six

Coming Full Circle

Having presented all applicable components of the discussion, it is now time to elucidate the complete purpose of the book. In order to fully obtain and realize the blessings God has in store for Black Americans, we MUST become a unit of people operating in solidarity. Solidarity is "unity or agreement of feeling or action, especially among individuals with a common interest; mutual support within a group" (dictionary.com). We as Black Americans have a common interest, and that is having a right, desire, and need of fully realizing equality, equity, justice, freedom, civil liberties, and equal access to wealth, health, education, and housing. And, of course, that list is *not* comprehensive. We desire and deserve all that is due unto us.

Looking once again at the Israelites, who achieved what God had in store for them (reaching the Promised Land), we can get a better understanding of how circumstances can go awry when people lack understanding of God's vision for them and when solidarity has not been achieved. One person going astray can certainly ruin an opportunity for a positive outcome for all.

When God instructed Moses, at the burning bush at Mount Sinai, to go back to Egypt and tell Pharaoh to let His people go, God meant all of His people. God did not desire for one person to be left behind.

At the end of a trying time in Egypt, with Pharaoh denying God's request due to his hardened heart and also the presence of the nine plagues (with the tenth on the horizon), a change was manifesting. Following God's instructions that had once again been provided through Moses, when the Israelites prepared for the Passover feast, everyone packed his/her belongings, ready to depart when the time came. Then, everyone engaged in the feast and placed the blood on the doorposts as directed, causing the lives of all the Israelites to be spared.

Upon leaving Egypt, the Israelites departed as *one* group. *No one* was left behind. Anytime you read or hear of the great Exodus, not a single Israelite has been said to have remained in Egypt – neither by choice nor neglect.

Then, while in the wilderness, through every task that was undertaken, the Israelites worked together; they camped together, they forged for food together, they worshipped together, etc. Was their togetherness harmonious? Absolutely not. All families fight, argue, and bicker. Nevertheless, they stayed together, demonstrating the mentality of "All for one, and one for all."

Then, after a journey of forty years in the wilderness, it came time to cross over the Jordan River to possess the Promised Land that God had prepared for their arrival. Allow me to paint the picture for you because that was where things began to fall apart, and the consequences of the Israelites' actions are long lasting - remaining evident even today.

When the Israelites approached the Jordan River, the physical barrier separating them from the Promised Land, they were still together and operating in solidarity. God's servant Moses had died and had been buried by God's own hand. Moses' minister and assistant Joshua had been granted the role of successor and was then leading the Israelites into their purpose, into their destiny.

After crossing the Jordan River, the Israelites were standing on the threshold of the Promised Land. As instructed, they went in to occupy what God had promised them. However, the land was inhabited by foreigners. So, the twelve tribes were required to enter the Promised Land and engage in many battles, to take over the land God had chosen for them, territory by territory.

After the battles were fought and the foreigners were driven out or slain, it was time to settle down and enjoy the promises of God. But only nine and a half tribes set up their homes in Canaan. The remaining two and a half tribes had other plans, which did not align with God's plan. They desired to remain on the eastern side of the Jordan River, setting up residence there. That was the first problem of many.

In Numbers 32, we read... *"The tribes of Reuben and Gad owned vast numbers of livestock. When they saw that the lands of Jazer and Gilead were ideally suited for their flocks and herds, they came to Moses, Eleazar the priest, and the other leaders of the community. They said, 'Notice the towns of Ataroth, Dibon, Jazer, Nimrah, Heshbon, Elealeh, Sibmah, Nebo, and Beon. The Lord has conquered this whole area for the community of Israel, and it is ideally suited for all our livestock. If we have found favor with you, please let us have this land as our property instead of giving us land across the Jordan River'."*

In Verse 33, we read that it was Moses who added the half tribe of Manasseh to Reuben and Gad, who had requested to remain on the east side of the Jordan. So, Moses was the one who assigned land to the tribes of Gad, Reuben, and half the tribe of Manasseh, the son of Joseph, on the eastern side of the Jordan. However, God's original plan was for the Israelites, yes, all of the Israelites, all twelve tribes, to inhabit Canaan - together. (Note- All of this occurred prior to the crossing of the Jordan and, of course, Moses' death. So, even before possessing Canaan, a plan to deviate from God's will was in the minds of two of the tribes.)

Let's take a brief pause to look at God's will, to gain a better understanding of what transpired. When discussing the will of God, there are at least two wills God operates in: His perfect will and His permissive will. I will say up front that there are many who do not subscribe to the idea of God's permissive will, stating God only has one will and equating a permissive will to being a powerless or weak entity. Also, others state a permissive will means God condones sinful choices. I, on the other hand, do believe in both wills and do not believe a permissive will is necessarily connected to sinful choices. I believe God's permissive will is operational when the will of humans is functional. Meaning, we are operating in our God-given right to choose.

The permissive will of God is what God permits/allows to occur in our lives rather than what He desires for us. We must fully understand the fact that just because God permits something does not mean it aligns with His perfect will. God is gentle and does not force anyone to follow His will; He gave everyone the power to choose. However, we must note that God's permissive will does not have the full blessings of His perfect will. Read the following example:

In 1 Samuel 8, God wanted to be the king of the Israelites, but the people saw how other nations had a natural king and desired one for themselves. They cried and complained to Samuel who went to God in prayer. God permitted them to have a king, even though that was not His perfect will for them. Was it wrong for the Israelites to have a king? No, but it was not a wise choice because who can serve as a better king than the creator Himself? Was it a sinful act to want and have a king? No, it was not. So, the Lord permitted the Israelites to have a human king. But, because that was not God's perfect will for the Israelites, problems were bound to occur. So, naturally, problems started. The Israelites experienced war after war. So, as you can see, the permissive will always has consequences. God knows what is best for us. When we choose to operate outside of God's plan, we can expect an undesired outcome.

Here is a modern-day example regarding God's will. There is a student who is graduating from high school with the plan to go to college. The student applies to multiple colleges and receives acceptance letters from two of them. The student chooses one of the two and attends there. It was God's perfect will for the student to attend the other college. God could have only allowed the student to receive an acceptance letter from the college He wanted the student to attend, orchestrating the student's path. However, that is not how God operates. In everything we do, God gives us a choice. If we consult God and lean not to our own understanding (Proverbs 3:5-6), we will make the choice that aligns with God's perfect will for our lives. However, if we choose the other option, it does not mean we will *not* achieve our desired outcome. But it may mean that there will be more struggles, and there may be additional challenges or setbacks.

So, as it relates to the college student, she will surely achieve her degree with perseverance and hard work, but she may not get the internship that lay in wait for her at the other college (a blessing God had in store) and she may not get hired at the firm of her choice by attending the alternate college (another attached blessing). Was her choice sinful? No. Did God permit her the option to choose? Yes.

Opposite of God's permissive will is the perfect will of God: God's divine plan for our lives. It is the plan He established for us before the foundation of the world. To operate in God's perfect will, we will need to be very patient and trust God, operating in our faith, and tuning our ears to hear what the Spirit of the Lord is saying to us, thereby giving us much-needed direction. God wants to give us His best, which has His full blessings, not the second best, which is usually what our personal choice provides us. Therefore, it is best to operate in God's perfect will - even when we do not fully understand it.

Why was it God's perfect will for all twelve tribes to co-exist together in the land of Canaan? What were the benefits of being unified? First of all, all twelve tribes living in proximity to each other would allow them the ability to worship at the tabernacle together and encourage one another in their faith and service to God. When we attempt to sojourn alone on our spiritual journey, without support from fellow believers, we find the journey arduous. Together, we provide support for one another, especially when we experience trials and difficulties in our lives.

Secondly, the Israelites could protect each other from foreign invasion. Just as when the Israelites entered Canaan and found it inhabited by foreigners, there were others who were always seeking to dwell there. Together, they were a formidable force against enemies. And, God would always be there to help them protect the land He had given them, as He had done in each battle they had fought and subsequently won.

Thirdly, they would be insulated from pagan influence by being a strong support system for continuing to function in the spiritual practices passed down from their forefathers. God had warned them about intermarrying with people who practiced different beliefs. God knew opposing belief systems would only cause the Israelites to stray away from Him. So, residing together while keeping foreigners out of the land would serve as a method of protection for the Israelites if they were together.

Take note of the following encounter, which led to battles being fought. When the Israelites were on their way to the Promised Land, two pagan kings raised up their armies against them. Amorite King Sihon and Og, the King of Bashan both challenged Israel and lost. Both of these kings had lived on the east side of the Jordan River...on the wrong side of the Jordan River. Remember, it was God's plan for the Israelites to inhabit the west side of the Jordan, together. So, even though the battles were won, as a result of God's favor, the battles were not necessary to be fought if the Israelites had not been interested in occupying that particular territory. Without having their eyes set upon the land on the east of the Jordan, the Israelites would have passed through the Amorites and the Bashanites without stirring up problems.

The people of Israel had to fight the armies of King Sihon and King Og because they were being attacked in a land that was not designated for them. The land these two kings had occupied was never part of God's plan for His people to occupy. It was just land they were to pass through on the way to the Promised Land.

But, two of the tribes became enamored with the looks of the east side of the Jordan. These two tribes had large herds of cattle and saw this territory as ideal for them. They bargained with Moses to return to that land and to remain in that land once all of Israel was secured in the Promised Land on the west side of the Jordan, where God wanted them. One Bible scholar puts it this way: "This decision by the Reubenites and Gadites was based on their lust to have what they saw as the most advantageous to themselves." How many times have we held a strong desire for something or someone that God did not design for us? And what happened when we strove after that desire? What was the final result?

Perhaps, the actions of the two tribes remind you of the story of Lot and Abraham. Genesis 13 records both Abraham and Lot having large flocks that the land could not support, so Abraham suggested they separate. Abraham operated in the spirit of grace, allowing Lot to choose first the land he desired to call home. The text tells us in Genesis 13:10-13, Lot looked around and saw that the whole plain of the Jordan toward Zoar was well watered, like the garden of the Lord, like the land of Egypt. (This was before the Lord destroyed Sodom and Gomorrah.) So, Lot chose for himself the whole plain of the Jordan and set out toward the east. The two men parted company: Abram lived in the land of Canaan, while Lot lived among the cities of the plain and pitched his tents near Sodom. Now, the people of Sodom were wicked and were sinning greatly against the Lord, and Lot positioned himself in close proximity of them.

Lot allowed his greed to direct his choice and evidently never gave thought to the fact that the land that he chose to live in was adjacent to wicked people who sinned greatly against the Lord. We, in making wise choices, should avoid being in close proximity to sin that is running rampantly.

It was a regrettable choice for Lot. Later, the people of Sodom and Gomorrah were destroyed because of their great sin, and Lot barely escaped himself, losing his wife in the process. *"Be not wise in thine own eyes: fear the LORD, and depart from evil,"* (Proverbs 3:7, KJV). The evil that is mentioned here is not necessarily evil that we are engaging in, but evil that may be near our location.

The decision that the two tribes made was very similar to Lot's decision. The allure of the fertile land was too intoxicating for them, so they (along with the half tribe assigned by Moses) separated themselves from the nine and a half tribes and lived with the Jordan River as a dividing line between them and their kin. The leaders of the tribes of Reuben, Gad and the half tribe of Manasseh believed their plan to isolate themselves on the east side of the Jordan was better than God's plan of keeping all twelve tribes together. It is not that they had the fortitude to compare their plan against God's plan, but even while knowing what God's plan was, they came up with an alternate plan.

It is one thing to be ill-informed about God's plan and not to patiently wait for it to be revealed. That in and of itself is not the best way to navigate through life, but it is far worse to know God's plan and choose an alternate one, as if we know better than God what is best for us. When we start believing that our plans are better than God's plans, consequences are just around the corner due to our regrettable choices.

Like many of us, the two and a half tribes saw the immediate benefit of the land they were *not* promised. They saw that it was ideally suited for them, from a practical perspective, despite what God wanted for them. They chose immediate blessings rather than delayed blessings. Sometimes, that is exactly what tempts us: what we "see" evident at that point as being readily available for us. What we "see" tends to move us more so than a promise that has yet to be activated.

One Bible scholar writes, "I have heard it said that 'what you focus on, you come to appropriate for yourself.' In the case of Reuben and Gad, they wanted what God had not planned for them. Was there no suitable pasture land on the west of the Jordan? They did not know, but they grabbed what looked good to them, perhaps on the 'I want it now' philosophy. Certainly, it was not in the perfect will of God. Were there consequences to this regrettable choice? Yes, there were."

Having remained on the eastern side of the Jordan, away from the remaining nine and a half tribes of Israel, away from God's tabernacle, they were vulnerable to attack by marauding bands and eventually, they also learned they were vulnerable to attack from the cruel king of Assyria.

In 740 B.C. Tiglath-Pileser, king of the great Assyrian empire, whose capital was a complex of four cities, carried away the Reubenites, the Gadites, and the half tribe of Manasseh, placing them as captive slaves in cities of Assyria. God's plan was to use the Assyrian captivity to teach the covenant people Israel how inexcusable was their disobedience. Just one generation earlier, Jonah had preached to Nineveh, and they repented. Forty years later, these same people exacted judgment on Reuben, Gad and the half tribe of Manasseh. Reuben, Gad and the half tribe of Manasseh chose earthly blessings over spiritual blessings, and they lost everything. They chose the 'good' rather than the 'best.' They settled for that which was readily available instead of the promised blessing.

Let's discuss the Assyrian captivity a bit further. When the Israelites were settled in Canaan (on both the east and west sides of the Jordan river), they were still a united people – *mentally, emotionally, and spiritually*. However, with a river separating nine and a half tribes from the other two and a half tribes, they were *physically* separated. As mentioned earlier, the physical separation caused a weakness in protecting all the people as one unit. When the attack by the Assyrians occurred on the eastern side of the Jordan, how was assistance from the western side of the Jordan supposed to be manifested with a river separating them? Remember, God had to part the waters to allow them passage. That means, the waters were not easily passable in human terms. It was not impossible, but if would take effort and time.

Years later, after having gone through a succession of kings and the death of King Solomon, the throne was in the hands of King Solomon's son Rehoboam. However, ten of the tribes (those located in the northern region) refused to submit to Rehoboam's authority. Their revolt against Rehoboam's throne eventually led to a division within the United Kingdom, creating two "states": the Kingdom of Israel (the northern kingdom) and the Kingdom of Judah (the southern kingdom). The Northern Kingdom of Israel was comprised of ten Hebrew tribes: Asher, Dan, Ephraim (half tribe), Gad, Issachar, Manasseh (half tribe), Naphtali, Reuben, Simeon, and Zebulun. Some tribes were on the western side of the Jordan river with the others on the eastern side. The Southern Kingdom of Judah was comprised of two tribes: Judah and Benjamin. The tribe of Levi was scattered throughout both regions.

Around 740 B.C., the two and a half tribes of the eastern side of the Jordan were "carried away" into captivity by the Assyrians. By 722 B.C., the remaining seven and a half tribes were taken into captivity by the Assyrians as well, creating what we now refer to as the "Lost Ten Tribes of Israel."

With their kin effectively being "gone," the Southern Kingdom of Judah was left with far less protection than before, making them susceptible to foreign invasion and attack as their kinfolk had been. Nearly one hundred years later, after the Assyrian attack in the north, Babylonia struck Judah in 625 B.C., asserting control with full power taken in 597 B.C., when nearly 10,000 Jews were taken to Babylon.

(Hooker, Richard. "The Hebrews: A Learning Module" Washington State University. Reviewed December 2020.)

What lesson can we as Black Americans learn from the Israelites' experiences? How do we apply what we have learned from their circumstances to ours? What I have attempted to demonstrate through the collective work of all six chapters is the power of solidarity and unification and how those two principles apply to God's desire to move Black Americans from our current position on the totem pole upward.

When the Lord wants to pour out His blessings on a group of people at the same time, they must be operating in concert. **That is the Lord's mandate.** If instead of operating in concert (with one mind, one vision, a solidified existence free from intraracial discrimination and prejudices), different segments of that particular group of people will function with its own ideologies, causing one segment of people to traverse one course while another segment is traversing another course and so on and so on. As a consequence, division will exist and different realities will be achieved instead of a singular reality- God's plan for the entire group.

Here is an example of one dissenter, operating within his own greed, who caused a terrible setback for the Israelites as a whole. Read the story of Achan.

The story of Achan is found in Joshua 7. God had delivered Jericho into the Israelites' hands, as recorded in Joshua 6. The Israelites had been instructed to destroy everything in the city, with the exception of Rahab and her family, as well as the city's gold, silver, bronze, and iron. The metals were to go into the tabernacle treasury; they were "sacred to the Lord" (Joshua 6:19) or "devoted" to Him. Jericho was to be totally destroyed, and the Israelites were to take no plunder for themselves.

Shortly after their success at Jericho, the Israelites moved on to attack the city of Ai. The spies Joshua sent to Ai thought the city would be easy to overtake—much easier than Jericho— and they suggested Joshua only send two or three thousand troops. Much to their shock, the Israelites were chased out of Ai, and thirty-six of them were killed. Joshua tore his clothes and bemoaned their attempts at conquering Canaan. He told God, "The Canaanites and the other people of the country will hear about this and they will surround us and wipe out our name from the earth. What then will you do for your own great name?" (Joshua 7:9). God responded by telling Joshua that some Israelites had sinned by taking devoted things. The people were to consecrate themselves, and then the following morning the perpetrator would be identified by lot (see Proverbs 16:33).

When morning came, each tribe presented itself. The tribe of Judah was chosen by lot, then the clan of the Zerahites, then the family of Zimri, then Achan. "Then Joshua said to Achan, 'My son, give glory to the Lord, the God of Israel, and honor him. Tell me what you have done; do not hide it from me'" (Joshua 7:19). Achan confessed his sin, admitting that in Jericho he saw a robe, two hundred shekels of silver, and a fifty-shekel bar of gold that he "coveted," took, and hid in a hole he had dug within his tent. Messengers from Joshua confirmed the plunder was found in Achan's tent, and they brought it before the assembly. The Israelites then stoned Achan, his children, and his livestock and burned the bodies; they also burned Achan's tent, the plunder he had taken, and "all that he had" in the Valley of Achor (i.e., the "Valley of Trouble"), Joshua 7:25–26. The pile of stones was left there as a reminder of Achan's sin and the high cost of not obeying the Lord.

After Achan was judged, God told Joshua, "Do not be afraid; do not be discouraged. Take the whole army with you, and go up and attack Ai. For I have delivered into your hands the king of Ai, his people, his city and his land" (Joshua 8:1). The Israelites laid an ambush and soundly defeated Ai, killing all of its inhabitants. This time, the Israelites were allowed to take the plunder for themselves. Only Jericho, the first city in Canaan, had been wholly devoted to the Lord (see Deuteronomy 18:4). The story of Achan is a stark reminder of the penalty of sin, which is death (Romans 6:23a). We also see two truths illustrated plainly: first, that sin is never an isolated event—our sin always has a ripple effect that touches others. Achan's sin led to the deaths of thirty-six of his fellow soldiers and defeat for the whole army. Second, we can always be sure that our sins will find us out (Numbers 32:23). Hiding the evidence in our tents will not conceal it from God.

Achan's sin was grave. He took what was God's. The Israelites had been specifically warned about the consequences of not doing as God instructed. Joshua told them, "Keep away from the devoted things, so that you will not bring about your own destruction by taking any of them. Otherwise you will make the camp of Israel liable to destruction and bring trouble on it" (Joshua 6:18). Achan's sin was a clear and willful violation of a direct order, and he did bring trouble on the entire camp of Israel. Also, Achan was given time to repent on his own; he could have come forward at any time, yet chose to wait through the casting of lots. Rather than admit his guilt and perhaps call on the mercy of God or at least demonstrate reverence for Him, Achan attempted to hide. "Whoever conceals their sins does not prosper, but the one who confesses and renounces them finds mercy" (Proverbs 28:13). The precious metals Achan took were meant to be given to the tabernacle; they were God's possession. So Achan not only disobeyed a direct order, but he stole from God Himself and then covered it up. The story of Ananias and Sapphira in Acts 5 is a similar warning against lying to God. As to why Achan's entire family was destroyed along with him, that is a bit difficult to understand. Most likely, they were complicit in the sin—they would surely have known about the hole dug in their tent and what was hidden there. Or perhaps their execution was a demonstration of just how pure the Israelites were called to be.

In the story of Achan we see just how deceptive sin can be. In the midst of a miraculous victory, Achan was enticed by a robe, some silver, and some gold—certainly none of that compares with the power of God he had just witnessed. Yet we know our own hearts can be just as easily swayed. James 1:14–15 says, "Each person is tempted when they are dragged away by their own evil desire and enticed. Then, after desire has conceived, it gives birth to sin; and sin, when it is full-grown, gives birth to death." Another aspect of sin's deception is that it promises a benefit that it just can't deliver. The stolen items did Achan absolutely no good; he couldn't spend the money, and he couldn't wear the clothes. What seemed of great worth to him was actually worthless, buried in a hole in the ground while guilt festered in his heart.

In Joshua 7:21, as Achan finally confesses his sin, he relates the process that led to his destruction: "I saw . . . I coveted . . . and took." This is the same process that leads to many sins today. Achan was deceived by sin's lies, but we don't have to be. "Don't be deceived, my dear brothers and sisters. Every good and perfect gift is from above, coming down from the Father of the heavenly lights, who does not change like shifting shadows. He chose to give us birth through the word of truth, that we might be a kind of firstfruits of all he created" (James 1:16-18).

Real blessing comes from God, not through the pleasures of sin. ("Who was Achan in the Bible." www.gotquestions.org/Achan-in-the-Bible. January 12, 2020. Reviewed December 28, 2020.)

Although the story focuses on sin quite a bit, my primary focus for sharing it with you is Achan's story demonstrates the consequences of departing from the group and going one's own way without regard to the wellbeing of the rest. If we as Black Americans do not heed the call for unification, we will not receive the blessings of God- as a unit. Please note, our individual blessings will remain intact, but God has so much more in store for us as a people. Will we not trust His word?

God had a singular plan for the Israelites. And beginning with hearing their cries, their moans, and their disgruntlements, God began to move on their behalf after they had suffered through a period of enslavement that lasted 400 years. However, in the midst of God effectuating His plan with efficient guidelines provided to the Israelites at each juncture of the process, the Israelites time and time again leaned to their own understanding.

Their leaning was the catalyst for God's plan going awry. God could have pushed back and placed barricades in their way, preventing them from taking an alternate course. But allowing them to operate in their free will, God permitted their choices. The Israelites on more than one occasion were referred to as a "stiff-necked people" (Ex. 32:9; 33:3, 5; 34:9; Deut. 9:6, 13; 10:16; 31:27; 2 Kings 17:14; 2 Chron. 30:8; Neh. 9:17, 29; Ps. 78:8; Jer. 7:26; 19:15). In the end, because they basically interfered with God's plan to fully orchestrate their destiny, they did not experience longevity in God's blessings.

Today, God wants to effectuate change in the lives of Black Americans to end their suffrage, which is a direct effect of slavery. The mistreatment Black Americans continuously suffer has been in existence for 500 years. God has heard our moans, our groans, and our cries. He has seen the bloodshed, the heinous crimes enacted upon and against us, the lynchings, the hangings, the bombings, the segregation, the injustices, the inequities, the inequalities, the subjugation, and the degradation. Through it all, He has recognized our strength, our efforts to manifest change, and our tenacity.

While the current condition of Black Americans is dissimilar to the Israelites in that we are not all located in one region of the United States and do not move around with one mentality, lifestyle, or resources, we are all situated in one context: life in the United States with our present situations being endured each and every day. Regardless of our differences with the Israelites, there are similarities between the two groups. Like the Israelites, Black Americans have a unified destiny, a historical plight, a culture steeped with tradition and beliefs (although much different from our original cultural traditions of the peoples of Africa), an abiding love for each other, strength, and endurance.

Another key factor that ties Black Americans together is most of the realities Black Americans face are inescapable regardless of the amount of money we may have in our bank account or the clothes with which we adorn our body. Simply put, no one is exempt from suffering the harsh treatments that are continuously inflicted upon us due to the color of our skin. Therefore, it is imperative that we understand the course we must prepare to embark upon is multifaceted, consisting of various components at once.

To effectuate the change God desires to initiate and complete on our behalf, we have work to do. We must permanently join forces, Black American with Black American, in order to work cohesively. It cannot be a *united front* as so many often use as a phrase to describe "togetherness." We must form a united coalition, one with an impenetrable infrastructure. A "front" refers to a presentation demonstrated for the benefit of others; whereas, a coalition represents a cohesive body of individuals solidified through love, vision, purpose, strength, and destiny, a body of people that is steadfast, unbreakable, and unrelenting, who are aligning themselves together for one purpose.

Sometimes, due to the inherent deceptions imbedded in American culture, we turn a blind eye to the reality of our situation when we see prosperity and growth in the ranks, such as one African American president who served for eight years in a long line of presidents who have collectively served for over two hundred years. Yes, we are a minority of people (13% of all Americans) having far less people compared to White Americans at 73%, but we have been in this land just as long, so why have we only had one Black president? Has there not been another person who was qualified to hold the highest political office of the land?

Also, there have been a few Black Americans who have broken through in terms of financial independence- particularly in entertainment- but that is not an accurate representation of what occurs in the lives of the majority of Black Americans.

Despite the progress we have seen, which cannot be denied, we are desirous of a leveled playing field - across the board. A playing field that includes equal access to all the same benefits others presently enjoy and sometimes take for granted.

Upon this leveled playing field,

We want to walk down the street or drive a vehicle without fear of being harassed or being shot and killed.

We want women to not have to worry about their Black sons, brothers, or husbands. Parents should not be required to have "the second talk" with their sons about how to function as a Black male in America in an effort to save their lives or to warn them about the prejudices they will undoubtedly face. Why should Black males or any Black person be required to respond differently in society to people in general, but specifically to sworn officers whose duty it is to protect and serve all people?

We want to apply for jobs and not be dismissed without being granted an interview because of the spelling or pronunciation of our names or from being viewed as an inferior candidate for employment.

We want to be welcomed into stores without the owners, who may have never set eyes on us before, thinking we are there to steal or that we cannot afford to purchase the items in stock. (Something that happened to Oprah Winfrey in a handbag boutique.)

We want to receive fair treatment in court cases and not be wrongly convicted or to receive harsher punishments than our white counterparts when crimes are committed.

We want our applications to purchase real estate or request a business loan to be seriously considered without prejudice.

Regardless of our current treatment by others and their lack of insight about how to treat all of humanity, God wants us to know who we are and how resilient we are.

Our **strength** is in numbers. Banded together, we can accomplish more. United we stand; divided we fall.

Our **strength** is in solidarity. If we walk with one voice, one vision, and one purpose, we can achieve our goals.

Our **strength** is in loving one another where we are, while working to strive for the betterment of all of us. Let's not degrade one another for what may be lacking. We have different backgrounds when it comes to being raised, educated, etc. Some of us had different opportunities than others. With different opportunities and experiences, we make and have made different choices. However, we can press forward together to create more opportunities for all of us.

Our **strength** is in whole heartedly believing that no person should be left behind. We must desire for a better tomorrow for all of us, not being satisfied with just some of us "making it over." We must have the "all or nothing" mentality. We are our brothers' and sisters' keepers.

Our **strength** is in not ignoring the struggle. We must be careful to not dismiss past struggles. Not sharing the past with our youth is one way of dismissing all we have been through and all we have achieved. Our struggles have made us who we are, and we are yet striving to overcome them, by fighting to not continue to live through them.

Our **strength** is in celebrating our accomplishments. We have made some great feats in history, attempting to overcome and right the wrongs that have been executed against us. Let's always celebrate our forerunners and the progress they have made.

Our **strength** is in lending a hand up to those who are disadvantaged, disenfranchised, and seemingly forgotten.

Our **strength** is in being change makers and not sitting idly by waiting for someone else to do the work. We must all put our hands to the plow.

Our **strength** is in positive thoughts and positive words. We are who we say we are. We must utter positive affirmations about ourselves and others, especially in public. Degrading one another gives others license to do the same. We cannot complain about what others say about us or call us if we are doing it to ourselves.

Using our **wants** as our motivating force and the collective set of **strengths** as our foundation, we are empowered to answer God's call. Right now, God is giving us a *Call to Action*, so we can prepare the necessary foundation to receive all He has in store for us. This country is based upon capitalism, a system of economic exchange. If one has sufficient currency to partake in the system, he/she will gain status and position, enabling him/her to have a seat at the table and to have a voice of authority. Without the tools to engage, one is rendered silent and powerless- to the margin of mainstream society.

That is the sole reason for the wealth transfer. God is preparing a seat at the table for us. He is preparing to shift the scales that have been improperly balanced for far too long.

There are many tables in our society. In many instances, Black Americans have had to create their own tables in order to have a seat. That's all fine and great, but why can't we sit at the head table to have a voice? We dispensed of the idea of 'separate but equal' that had been attempted to be substantiated through Plessy v Ferguson long ago. We know that separate is not always equal, so why buy into that ideology now?

Let's prepare to take a seat at the head table by following God's direction to come together. From there, God will do the rest. He will transfer much-needed wealth into our hands. And, we, while operating appropriately with the funds to sustain our wealth, will sit at the table and have a voice in making changes that support equality, equitable treatment, lawfulness, proper housing, educational advancements, and employment opportunities.

It is not too late to see the manifestation of the dream of an African-American King - Dr. Martin Luther King, Jr. He stated in his 1963, "Letter from Birmingham Jail," that tension is necessary to help men *"rise from the dark depths of prejudice and racism to the majestic heights of understanding and brotherhood."* We must be willing to do all that is necessary to effectuate change, and it may not all be pretty or warm and fuzzy. However, we must do in it in a positive manner, one that is pleasing to God. Taking one action at a time, we will get there.

*My brothers and sisters, God wants to do something **for** us, but it will **not** happen until He does something **within** us!*

Once we do as God has directed, He will do the rest!

Are you ready?

The Last

Shall Be

First

Chapter Seven

A Closing Thought

This book is filled with a wealth of information and a God-given prophetic directive. While it may be much to ingest, it is necessary to take it all in. To make it more palatable, allow me to share with you an encounter I had with the Lord the day before I finished the book.

On Sunday mornings, between worship services, I teach the women's Sunday school class at my place of worship. On the last Sunday of the year, December 27, 2020, as I was beginning class, Holy Spirit began to move, making His presence known- at least to me. Now, that in and of itself is nothing new. Each week, Holy Spirit is present to guide me through the class, using me as a vessel to speak to, teach, and encourage the women.

On that Sunday, however, His presence was literally over-whelming. For the past several Sundays, I had been encouraging the women to pray for all our congregants' health and wellbeing. Also, I had asked them to pray for our country as our land was continuing to be hit hard with COVID-19 cases and deaths. One such death had occurred that was near and dear to me and my family. In the midst of me asking them to pray, the Lord began to speak, telling me to tell the women, "Change is coming. It is imminent, and the things we are suffering now will not last always."

Then, the Lord said the pandemic had to come to shake things up, flip them upside down, and to knock some things loose. The pandemic was necessary to open eyes. Through all the Lord was speaking to me at the moment to share with the women, He was also speaking directly to me. He was re-affirming the prophecy He had given me to write and share with all of you through this book. The Lord was informing me that a change is coming within our nation that will be manifested in the lives of Black Americans, which will impact the entire American nation.

God is ready to bring much-needed change to our nation. Are you ready for it? Are you ready to fulfill your responsibility? Are you ready to walk in the newness of life?

Change is coming! It is on the horizon!

The Last Shall be First, because God has the final word!

References

Alonso, A. (2010). "Out of the Void." In Hunt, Darrell; Ramos, Ana-Cristina (eds.). *Black Los Angeles: American Dreams and Racial Realities.* New York City: NYU Press.

"American Civil Rights." www.gettysburgflag.com/timeline-american-civil-rights. Retrieved December 1, 2020.

Barnes, Albert. *Notes on the Whole Bible.* (1832). London: Blackie and Son Publishers.

"Black Panthers." History.com Editors. www.history.com. November 3, 2017. Accessed on December 7, 2020.

Busey, C. L. (2014). "Examining Race from Within: Black Intraracial Discrimination in Social Studies Curriculum." *Social Studies Research and Practice. Vol. 9*(2). www.socstrp.org.

Callimachi, R. "Breonna Taylor's Family to Receive $12 Million Settlement from City of Louisville." nytimes.com. September 15, 2020. Reviewed on November 30, 2020.

Dedel, K. (2007). "The Problem with Drive-By Shootings." Problem-Oriented Guides for Police, Problem-Specific Guide No. 47. Washington, D.C.: U.S. Department of Justice, Office of Community Oriented Policing Services.

"Emmet Till is Murdered." history.com. August 28, 1955. Reviewed on November 30, 2020.

Encyclopedia.com. "House Slaves an Overview." 2019. Accessed December 9, 2020.

Harris, D. (2004). *Gangland.* Goose Creek, South Carolina:

Holy Fire Publishing. p. 49. Reviewed December 16, 2020.

Hill, E. "How George Floyd was Killed in Police Custody." nytimes.com. May 31, 2020. Reviewed on November 30, 2020.

History.com Editors. "Jim Crow Laws." February 18, 2018. History.com. Accessed December 6, 2020.

Hooker, R. "The Hebrews: A Learning Module." Washington State University. Reviewed December 2020.

Hunt, Darnell & Ramon, Ana-Christina. (May 2010). *Black Los Angeles*. Reviewed December 16, 2020.

Jackson, D. A. (2017). "The Lasting Legacy of the 1992 Watts Gang Truce." www.atlantablackstar.com. Reviewed December 16, 2020.

Johnson, J. H. (Editor). "Black on Black Crime - The Cause, The Consequences, The Cures." *Ebony Vol. 34*(10). (1978). Retrieved December 9, 2020.

King, Martin Luther, Jr. (1963). *Why We Can't Wait.* Penguin Group, Inc.: New York.

LAPD Online. "Why Young People Join Gangs." www.lapdonline. Accessed December 16, 2020.

Machado, J. & Turner, K. "6 Myths About Black People in American." Feb. 18, 2020. www.vox.com/identities. Reviewed on Dec. 10, 2020.

MSU Billings Library. "African-American Rights Movements: Legislation / Court Cases." https://libguides.msubillings.edu. December 5, 2019. Accessed December 6, 2020.

Munro, A. "The Shooting of Trayvon Martin." June 29, 2015. Reviewed on November 30, 2020.

"NAACP History: Medgar Evers." naacp.com. 2020. Reviewed on November 30, 2020.

"NAACP Timeline." sutori.com and thoughtsco.com. Reviewed December 2020.

Obama, Barack. (2020). *A Promised Land.* Crown Publishers: New York.

Peralta, S. (Director), Stacy Peralta & Sam George (writers), Baron Davis et al. (producer), Steve Luczo, Quincy "QD3" Jones III (executive producer) (2009). *Crips and Bloods: Made in America* (TV-Documentary). PBS Independent Lens series. Retrieved December 16, 2020.

Perry, M. J. "The shocking story behind Richard Nixon's 'War on Drugs' that targeted blacks and anti-war activists." (2018). aei.org. Retrieved December 9, 2020.

"President Barack Obama." The White House. 2008. Archived from the original on October 26, 2009. Reviewed December 2020.

Riechmann, D. "Trump blasts 4 congresswomen; crowd roars, 'Send her back!'" July 18, 2019. Reviewed on November 30, 2020.

Riphagen, L. "Marginalization of African-Americans in the Social Sphere of Us Society." The Interdisciplinary Journal of International Studies Vol. 5. (2008) Reviewed December 9, 2020.

Sharkey, Betsy (2009-02). "Review: 'Crips and Bloods: Made in America'." *Los Angeles Times.* Retrieved December 16, 2020.

Sloan, Cle. (Director). Antoine Fuqua and Cle Sloan (producer),

Jack Gulick (executive producer) (2009). Keith Salmon (ed.). *Bastards of the Party* (TV-Documentary). HBO. Retrieved December 16, 2020.

Stinson, P. & Wentzlof, C. (2019). "On-Duty Shootings: Police Officers Charged with Murder or Manslaughter, 2005-2019." Accessed November 2020.

Stoltze, F. (April 28, 2012). "Forget the LA Riots – historic 1992 Watts gang truce was the big news." *89.3 KPCC Southern California Public Radio*. Retrieved December 16, 2020.

"Timeline: South Central Los Angeles." PBS (part of the "Crips and Bloods: Made in America" TV documentary). April 21, 2009. Retrieved December 16, 2020.

Turan, Cyan. June 19, 2020. cosmopolitan.com. Reviewed December 1, 2020.

"Who was Achan in the Bible." www.gotquestions.org/Achan-in-the-Bible. January 12, 2020. Reviewed December 28, 2020.

Williams, Heather Andrea. "How Slavery Affected African American Families." Freedom's Story, TeacherServe©. National Humanities Center. Accessed on December 15, 2020. www.nationalhumanitiescenter.org.

Williams, Stanley Tookie; Smiley, Tavis (2007). *Blue Rage, Black Redemption*. Simon & Schuster. pp. xvii–xix, 91–92, 136. Reviewed December 16, 2020.

Gift of Salvation

for Non-Believers

"For all have sinned, and come short of the
glory of God."
(Romans 3:23)

This section was written especially for non-believers, those who have not accepted the gift of salvation. The gift of salvation saves souls from eternal damnation and is a free gift offered by God himself.

John 3:16-18 says, *"For God so loved the world, that he gave his only begotten Son, that whosoever believeth in him should not perish, but have everlasting life. For God sent not his Son into the world to condemn the world; but that the world through him might be saved. He that believeth on him is not condemned: but he that believeth not is condemned already, because he hath not believed in the name of the only begotten Son of God."*

This section of scripture tells us God's purpose for giving His son Jesus to the world. The world was in a bad condition. The world was overwrought with sin; the people were living for fleshly desires rather than for God's desires.

As a result of the world's conditions, God decided He would offer the perfect sacrifice that would save the world from being a place where people were lost and had no hope. He decided that His own son could stand in proxy for the sin-filled world, taking all sin upon Himself.

So Jesus came, born of a virgin, to save this dying world. He walked on this earth for 33 ½ years, doing the work of His Heavenly Father. At the appointed time, He died by way of crucifixion upon a cross at Calvary, on Golgatha's hill. He shed his blood and died for you and for me. Because His blood was pure, it paid the penalty for all unrighteousness and gave those who believe in Him direct access to His father's throne.

Scripture tells us in Matthew 27:51 that the veil of the temple was ripped in two from top to bottom, at the moment that Jesus' spirit left His body. As a result of the veil's removal, we are no longer required to have a high priest make intercession for us. We, as the children of the Most High God, are able to approach the throne God for ourselves, and Jesus sits on the right hand of the Father making intercession for us.

But what is even more miraculous than God offering His own son as the perfect sacrifice was the fact that when Jesus was placed in grave clothes and placed in a tomb, He only remained there until the third day. God would not have it that His son would remain in the heart of the earth forever. In order for people to believe in the awesome power of God and His dear son Jesus, a miracle had to be performed. So, on the third day, after Jesus died on the cross, He was resurrected, demonstrating the omnipotence of God. This very act was the act that would cause people to believe in a god that reigns supreme and holds the power of the universe in His very hands, a god that could save them from themselves.

Today, if you are an unbeliever, you can change your destiny. You can change where you will spend your eternity. Our Heavenly Father gives us the freedom of choice about how we want to live our life here on earth and how we want to spend eternity. In Deuteronomy 30:19, God boldly declares, *"I call heaven and earth to record this day against you, that I have set before you life and death, blessing and cursing: therefore choose life, that both thou and thy seed may live."*

So, dear friend what choice will you make today? Will you spend your eternity with the Creator or will you suffer Hell's eternal flames?

Again, the choice is yours. Just as the men aboard the ship who were with Jonah became believers, you too can make a choice to accept the only one and true living God as your god.

If after reading the above passages, you have decided that you want to spend your eternity in Heaven with God, the creator, and His son Jesus, and Holy Spirit, read through what has affectionately come to be known as the Roman's Road. This is the road to salvation. As you read through the scriptures that comprise the Roman's Road, you will also read the explanation for each scripture so you will have clarity about what you are reading and confessing.

The Roman's Road to Salvation

The road to salvation begins with Romans 3:23 which declares, *"For all have sinned, and come short of the glory of God."* This scripture explains that everyone has come short of God's glory and needs redemption. Then Romans 6:23a states, *"For the wages of sin is death."* Here, we learn that the consequence of living a life of sin is death. Everyone will experience physical death as a result of the sin committed in the garden of Eden, but those who commit themselves to a life of sin will suffer eternal damnation in the lake of fire (Rev. 19).

Continue with the rest of verse 6:23 that says, *"but the gift of God is eternal life through Jesus Christ our Lord."* There is an alternative to suffering eternal damnation. We can accept the gift of salvation by accepting Jesus as our personal lord and savior. Then, Romans 5:8 says, *"But God commendeth his love toward us, in that, while we were yet sinners, Christ died for us."* We are able to receive the gift of salvation because Christ came to earth and shed His blood for us on the cross.

Continue to Romans 10: 9-10 which says, *"That if thou shalt confess with thy mouth the Lord Jesus, and shalt believe in thine heart that God hath raised him from the dead, thou shalt be saved. For with the heart man believeth unto righteousness; and with the mouth confession is made unto salvation."* If we confess with our mouths that Jesus is the son of God, that he came and died for our sins, and that God raised Him from the dead, we will receive salvation.

Finish with Romans 10:13, which states, *"For whosoever shall call upon the name of the Lord shall be saved."* Call upon the name of God by saying these words, **"Lord Jesus, come into my heart and save me Lord. I believe that you are the Son of God who came and died on the cross for my sins. I believe that you rose from the grave. I also believe that you now sit in heaven on the right side of the Father, making intersession for me. I accept you as my Lord and my Savior."**

Now that you have confessed with your mouth that Jesus is the son of God and that He died for our sins and rose from the grave, **YOU ARE NOW SAVED!!!!** You will spend your eternity in heaven.

The next step is very important- you must find a Bible-based church that teaches the word of God and confesses the Lord Jesus Christ to be the son of God. Don't delay. Do this immediately. Do not leave yourself open to the enemy. Get connected with the saints of the Most High God and keep yourself covered with the unspotted blood of the lamb.

Here is my prayer for you.

Father God,

I thank you for the opportunity to minister your word to the unsaved, the unchurched, and the uncommitted. Father God, I pray now for the souls who have just received the gift of salvation. Lord

Father, they have opened their hearts to you, and I know that you have received them into your kingdom and written their names in the Book of Life. Father God, I pray that you will touch their lives and show yourself mightily before them. Let their eyes be opened by the scales falling off, allowing them to see clearly.

Father God, I even pray for the backslider, those who have turned away from you after receiving the gift of salvation. You said in your word that you desire that none would perish. So Lord, I send your word to them right now praying that they would confess the iniquity in their heart, repent, and turn from their evil ways, so that they may receive a life of abundance. You said in your word in Matthew Chapter 14, that every knee shall bow before you and every tongue will confess that Jesus is Lord.

Father God, I pray now that we all come under subjection to your word and that we will humbly submit our lives to you. I ask all these things in the name of my Lord and Savior Jesus Christ. Amen, Amen, Amen!!!!

I will continue to pray for your success in your walk with God. Remember, this spiritual walk that you are about to embark on will not be an easy walk, but remember, the race is not given to the swift but to those who endure to the end.

Be blessed with heaven's best. I love you!

OTHER BOOKS BY THE AUTHOR
(All books can be purchased at www.creativemindsbookstore.com)

From Despair, through Determination, to Victory!

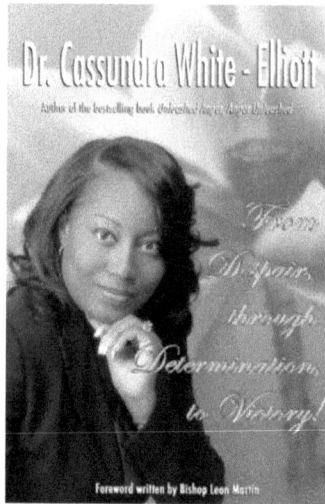

A lot can happen during a span of 40 years. The life of Dr. Cassundra White-Elliott has been anything but uneventful. From a fun-loving childhood sprinkled with incidents of abuse to a tumultuous young adulthood to a stable, secure adult life, she has experienced a full life, with much more to come. Her story is inspiring and motivating.

If anyone lacks hope, reading Dr. White-Elliott's autobiography will propel him/her into an attitude of "Maybe I can." This attitude, if nurtured and developed, will grow into an attitude of "Yes, I can." Throughout her life, Dr. White-Elliott has always held in her heart the belief that she could achieve anything that she had a made-up mind to embark upon. She was determined to achieve her heart's desires, doing what God has called her to do. She takes no credit for herself. All the glory goes to God, for He is her driving force. In Him, she lives, moves, and has her being.

Through the Storm

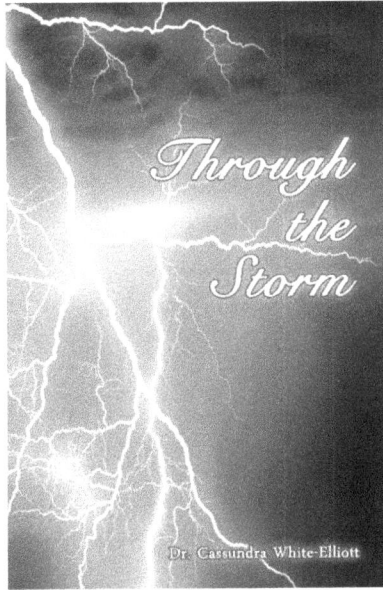

Through the Storm was duly inspired by the avaricious cloud of depression that decided to hover overhead of my daily existence in the latter part of 2007. Although I found it extremely difficult, I was once again compelled to not be defeated by just another snare that the enemy, the trickster, set for me. Once again, or more appropriately I should say *continuously*, he has exerted pernicious efforts to snatch the very life out of me by causing me to wallow in despair and to believe that I had been overcome by failure when in actuality and all reality, I was just experiencing a temporary setback. During those cloudy days, I had to remind myself daily that even though I was a target of the enemy, I am and will always be a child of the Most High God, Jehovah, who is my rock, my stability.

Unleashed Anger, Anger Unleashed

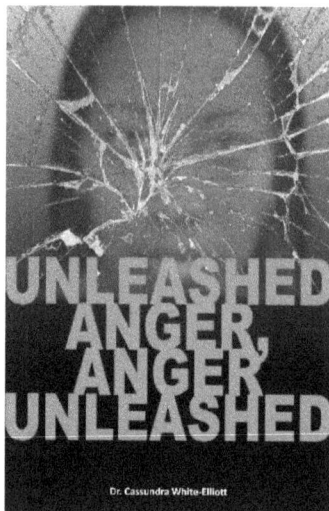

Introduction
What Is This Book All About?

As I prepared to embark upon the adventure of writing this book, I had to prepare myself to also be transparent. I have found that being transparent is required in order for healing to transpire, healing for all those that peruse the pages of this book and myself. And I may as well tell you that today, at the onset of this project, I have not been totally delivered from my condition of being an anger-filled person. However, I am definitely a work in progress. I have made strides with the assistance of my Lord and Savior, Jesus Christ, who is the head of my life. Without his love, guidance, and teachings, I would not be the woman of God I am today. I shudder to think where I could be instead and will therefore not entertain the thought.

Public Speaking in the Spiritual Arena

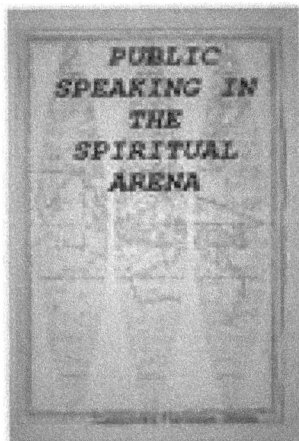

Chapter Two
How Communication Works
Purpose: This chapter will explain the six primary components of communication, identifying their purpose and how they work together.

The Source

In oral communication, the source of information is the speaker. In a church setting, the foundation of the message is God's word, but it is a speaker's interpretation of God's word that is delivered to the audience. As speakers vary, the information may vary but should have a similar essence because the foundational text is the same.

The Message

The message is the collective set of ideas that the speaker (the source) wants to deliver and/or illustrate to the audience. The message can be informative where the speaker informs the audience about a specific set of information. Or, the message may be persuasive in nature if the speaker wants to persuade the audience about conducting themselves in a specific manner, accepting God's commandments, or any number of things.

Where is Your Joppa?

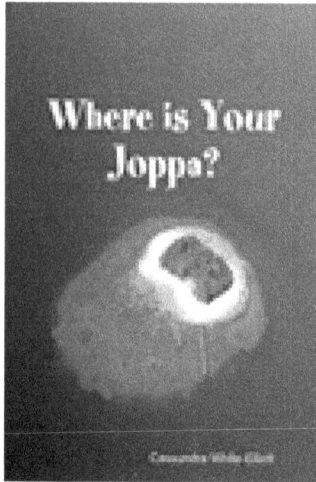

Introduction

Where is Your Joppa? was written for the express purpose of illustrating God's call for obedience in the lives of believers with respect to the individual call that He has on each of our lives. As you read throughout the various chapters, notice that the emphasis is placed on our persistent disobedience in answering God's call in a specific area of our lives. We have become a people who are similar to the Israelites when they found themselves in the middle of the wilderness, following their exodus from Egypt. Before God, they murmured and complained about their current life conditions and failed to be obedient to God's statutes delivered through His servant Moses. Their persistent disobedience caused them to lose the opportunity to see and enter the Promised Land. I ask you, "What has your disobedience cost you?" "Was your disobedience worth what it cost you?" "Do you think about the souls you could have ushered into the kingdom of God?" These are some of the questions that I pray will be answered through your reading of the book.

Mayhem in the Hamptons

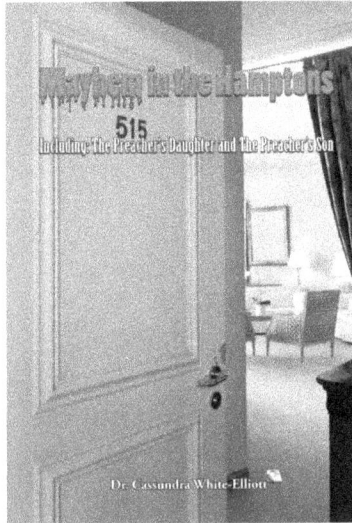

Romero and Yolanda optimistically plan for the day that is going to change their lives from being single persons to a couple who is united in holy matrimony. They, along with their parents, close friends and family, fly over to the infamous Hamptons, where only the rich and famous vacation, to have their dream wedding at the five-star Hampton Suites located on a peninsula in the Hamptons. Little do they know that their perfect day will turn out to be less than perfect when their wedding planner Mariesha Coleman suddenly goes missing!

A time when the newlyweds' lives should be filled with joy and the creation of wonderful memories, they are stricken with grief as they desperately try to find clues to help solve Mariesha's disappearance.

Mayhem in the Hamptons is a tale that shares how the horrors of a woman's past can come back to haunt her in more than one way and the impact it can have on anyone who gets in the way.

Preacher's Daughter

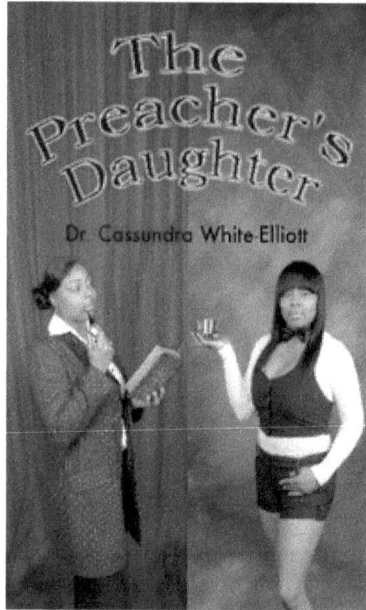

Tinisha, the daughter of a preacher, is a twenty-six-year-old God-fearing young woman endeavoring to complete law school so that she can make her mark in the courtroom. Working in one of the late-night clubs in Hollywood to earn money to pay her own way through school, Tinisha soon learns that life doesn't always go as planned. Finding her strength in her faith, Tinisha constantly finds herself praying as she watches God move miraculously in her life.

Preacher's Son

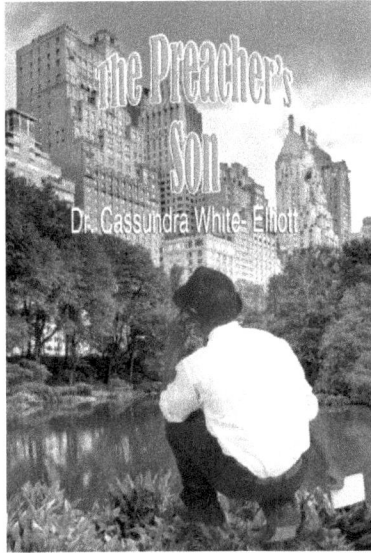

Romero Turner is a private investigator with a promising future. As he continues to build his career, he is excited about the cases he undertakes. However, his father Pastor Theodore Turner has other plans for his son's life. In the midst of trying to save his client's husband from Sylvester Domingo, a ruthless crime lord, Romero must try to salvage his relationship with his father. He must decide if ministry or life as a detective is in his future.

Lord, Teach Me to be a Blessing!

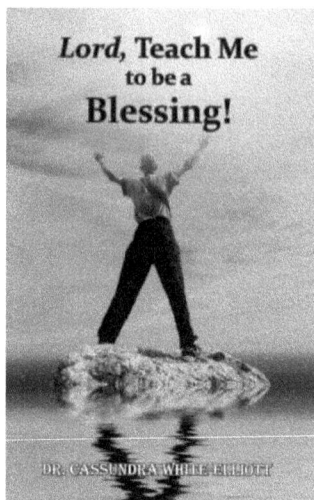

Lord, Teach Me to be a Blessing! will change a person's mentality from being centered around "me, myself, and I" to focusing on "others."

The world system teaches us that it is acceptable to place ourselves above others in an attempt to get ahead and even to survive. Herbert Spencer coined the phrase '*survival of the fittest*' after reading Charles Darwin's theory of evolution. This concept of surpassing and outdoing others is the world's philosophy.

However, the word of God does not subscribe to or promote this self-centered ideology, and therefore, neither should believers. We must hold fast to the truths outlined in Holy Scripture: "*Love thy neighbor as you love thyself*" (James 2:8) and "*It is more blessed to give than to receive*" (Acts 20:35).

While holding God's truths to be self-evident, we must demonstrate them to others, thereby showing them the way of the Lord of how to be a blessing to someone *rather* than looking to receive a blessing.

This is the very purpose of this book: to change the mentality of the world from being *self*-centered to *other* centered.

After the Dust Settles

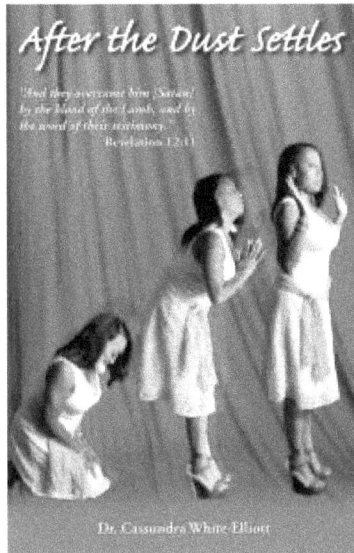

Throughout the journey of life, we all experience ups and downs and joys and pains. Most of us successfully find solutions to the situations/problems we encounter, but we often avoid dealing with the attached emotions. If we continue to ignore the emotions of pain, hurt, disappointment, anger, etc., we set ourselves up for destruction. Our families, our cultures, and our society tell us to be strong, to keep our chin up, and to grin and bear it. However, these methods of avoidance can lead us to strokes due to the undue amount of pressure we place on ourselves and/or mental illness from being unable to cope with the emotional baggage we have accumulated.

In *After the Dust Settles,* Dr. C. White-Elliott shares several situations that we all may encounter at one time or another in our lifetime and how to successfully navigate through them, so we can find ourselves emotionally healthy after the dust has settled and the situation has been rectified.

Begin reading today and experience a better tomorrow!

Claim Your Inheritance

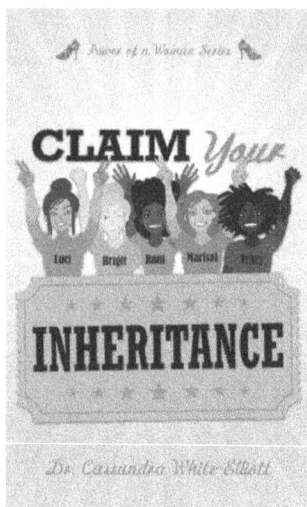

"The thief cometh not, but for to steal, and to kill, and to destroy: I am come that they might have life, and that they might have it more abundantly" (John 10:10).

Satan's mission is to steal, kill, and destroy all that God has provided for us. With him on the rampage, we must be ready to go to war-spiritually and naturally. On the other hand, we could sit idly by and allow the enemy to take what is rightfully ours. However, that is not the will of God. God has given us power to tread upon serpents and scorpions (Luke 10:19) and to reclaim all the enemy has stolen from us.

This book will share how we can be victorious in reclaiming what is rightfully ours when the enemy has turned his ugly head in our direction and made us prey for his latest scheme.

With God on our side, the enemy will not prevail!

A Diamond in the Rough

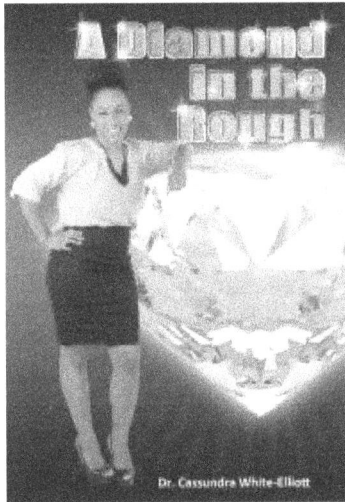

A Diamond in the Rough Architecture Firm was built and is owned and operated by lead architect Kyra Fraser. For the last five years, Kyra has been extremely successful in business, but her love life leaves much to be desired.

Kyra has set high standards for herself and does not wish to take a man in any condition and attempt to make him over. She is looking for someone who is drama free, well educated, very cultured, fun-loving, good looking, self-motivated, and the list goes on.

Will Kyra find the man of her dreams, or will her dream just continue to be a dream?

As you delve into this page-turning novel, Kyra's reality will unfold as you are drawn into her world of design, love and office drama- which includes her best friend's husband who is looking for love in all the wrong places.

365 Days of Encouragement

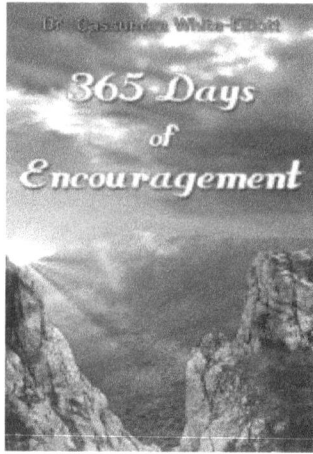

Just as our brain requires oxygen obtained from the air we breathe to sustain our mortal bodies, our spirit requires revitalization and encouragement in order to be strengthened each and every day of our lives. The revitalization and encouragement needed for the spirit of man comes directly from the word of God and assists us in walking according to the way of our heavenly Father. 365 Days of Encouragement provides a scripture a day for each day of the year. Along with the daily scripture is a brief note of commentary also for the benefit of edifying the saints of God.

It is my prayer that the people of God would live a fulfilled life through Christ Jesus. Knowing His word and understanding we can walk in the fulfillment thereof is empowering. We are instructed in II Timothy 2:15, "Study to shew thyself approved unto God, a workman that needeth not to be ashamed, rightly dividing the word of truth" (KJV). Take an opportunity to delve further into the word of God, to know His statutes and to allow your own personal life to be edified, so you can be equipped to bring glory to God and lived a fulfilled life.

A Mother's Heart

A Mother's Heart shares the unconditional love of mothers through a compilation of testimonies. Each testimony serves as a tribute to a special mother. The children of the represented mothers have lovingly written about their childhood, young adult life and/or older adult experiences they shared with their mother. As you read the writers' reflections, you will feel the expressions of love exude from the pages.

The purpose of this book is two-fold. First, it honors those mothers who stood by their children through the trials of life and showered them with unconditional love. Second, the book is a source of encouragement for mothers who may feel inadequate and question whether or not they are actually suited for motherhood. Our advice to mothers is, "Be encouraged; the journey of motherhood may seem daunting at times and you may shed some tears, but your children will never forget the love you have shown them and instilled in them to share with others."

Mothers may not be perfect, but they are definitely unmatched by any other category of person on God's green earth!

Broken Chains

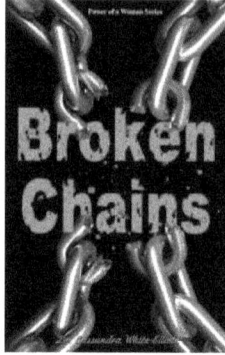

Broken Chains is an in-depth survey of five life-changing tragedies that can and will serve as chains to bind us if we are not watchful and mindful of their potential effects. In our lifetimes, we may all experience death of loved ones, sexual abuse, broken relationships, promiscuity, and sickness and disease. These everyday life occurrences can have detrimental effects on the remaining years of our lives and change our existence, unless we deal with them in a healthy manner.

Broken Chains not only brings to light the detrimental effects of five life-changing tragedies, but it also shares how anyone who experiences them can be healed and delivered from their effects.

If you have experienced death of a loved one, sexual abuse, a broken relationship, the effects of promiscuity, and/or sickness and disease and have not been able to rid yourself of the emotions attached to them or specific resulting behaviors, Broken Chains is for you.

God designed each of us for a purpose, and He has an intended end for us to achieve. In order for us to effectively achieve our God-given purpose, we must be free of chains that bind us. It is not God's desire that we become immobilized by life's events. His desire is for us to be healed, delivered and set free. Be healed today, in the name of the Lord Jesus Christ!

I Have Fallen

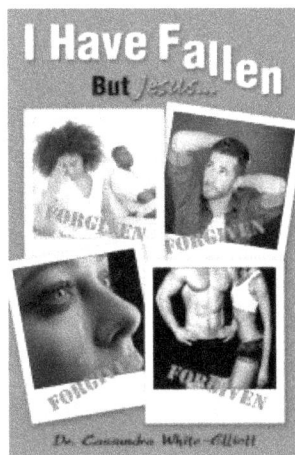

Do you know anyone who has committed his/her life to Christ but has done something unseemly that you would never expect a Christian to do? How did you feel about that person or what the person did? Did you pass judgment? What if that person were you? How would you feel if you made a misstep and no one forgave you and instead began to treat you differently? How do you feel when you are judged for past mistakes or lifestyles that are no longer part of your life?

This book shares four true stories of Christians who have made missteps during their walk with God. The purpose is not to air their dirty laundry, but to demonstrate our humanness and our vulnerability. None of us are exempt from making errors and falling into sin. It can happen to any of us.

The solution for these dilemmas is for the person who fell into sin to make a life-changing move and turn away from the sin, repent and ask God for forgiveness. His arms are waiting!

The next solution is for those who witness the sin or know of it. Pray and be of comfort to the one who has fallen. Lead him/her back to the path of righteousness. Love thy neighbor and treat him/her as you want to be treated!

The Bottom Line

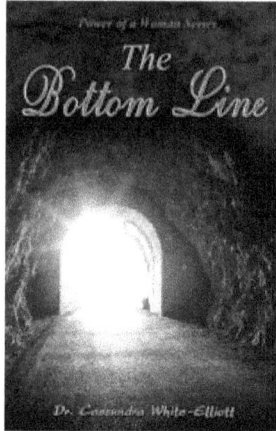

The Bottom Line is a detailed review of the Book of Job. Much can be said about Job's experiences with the loss of his children and wealth and the subsequent return of it all in mass proportions. However, the telling of Job's story in the Holy writ was not intended to focus on the return of his wealth. Instead, the focal point should be on the bottom line of the entire situation.

When you experience trials or tragedies in your life, do you tend to focus on the trial itself, the result, or the bottom line?

"What is the bottom line?" you may ask. The bottom line is the message God is sending regarding the situation.

When Job experienced his tragedies, there was a bottom line. Likewise, when you experience your trials and tragedies, there is a bottom line as well. It is up to you to discover it.

This book will reveal the bottom line in the Book of Job. It is readily apparent, but many often overlook it.

Now, it is up to you to uncover the bottom line of your experiences, for God will not bring a trial to you without a good reason.

Power of a Woman Series

Time is Running Out!

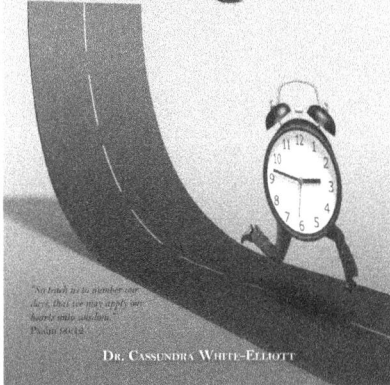

"So teach us to number our
days, that we may apply our
hearts unto wisdom."
Psalm 90:12

DR. CASSUNDRA WHITE-ELLIOTT

Every born-again believer has a God-given assignment. Whether or not the individual accepts the assignment is a personal decision. For those who choose to walk in God's will rather than their own must then follow God's divine plan for their life. Completing the God-given assignment means tuning one's ear to hear, receiving guidance, knowing when to commence, and, most importantly, exercising patience. Furthermore, the task may require enduring hardship along the way. A servant of the Lord can never fully anticipate what may occur during the journey of completing an assignment. What should be foremost in the individual's mind is completing the task, so he/she can hear the Master say, "Well done.".

If you have never completed a God-given assignment, or if you are preparing to embark upon a new journey designed by the Lord, this book is for you. It will provide guidance for commencing and completing God-given tasks. If you feel intimidated by the task ahead, don't be dismayed. The Lord said He will never leave you or forsake you (Hebrews 13:5). Trust and believe that He will be with you every step of the way.

But you must act now!
Time is running out!

CLF Publishing, LLC.
www.clfpublishing.org

ISBN 978-1-945102-23-9
90000

Dr. Cassundra White-Elliott's books are available at
www.creativemindsbookstore.com
www.amazon.com
www.barnesandnoble.com

9 781945 102219

Power of a Woman

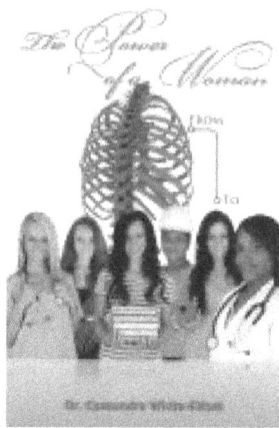

The ongoing conversation about the value of a woman is presented from a different perspective in The Power of a Woman. Dr. Cassundra White-Elliott presents a biblical perspective of women and compares it to the worldview of both yesterday and today. This comparison seeks to illustrate God's intended purpose for His uniquely designed creation: woman. Dr. Elliott shares God's truth about pre-imposed limitations set by man versus the limitations God Himself set for woman in addition to the wealth of liberality He gave her.

Women's creativity and abilities are not meant to be stifled. They are meant to be utilized to bring glory to God, to help sustain and nurture their families, and to move the world forward. Knowing God's truth will show women how to celebrate and appreciate who they are as well as one another!

Women, let's take the blinders off, lift our heads up, and march forward, side by side with men, and bring glory and honor to God! Take your rightful place with a gentle smile and grace and be who God called you to be!

Set Free

If you possess habits and display characteristics that are unbecoming, debilitating, and hinder the desired progress in your life or that affect your relationships with others, Set Free will provide the steps you need to be healed and delivered, through the Word of God.

Deliverance is available to you! Claim your healing today and walk in victory!

Do You Know God?

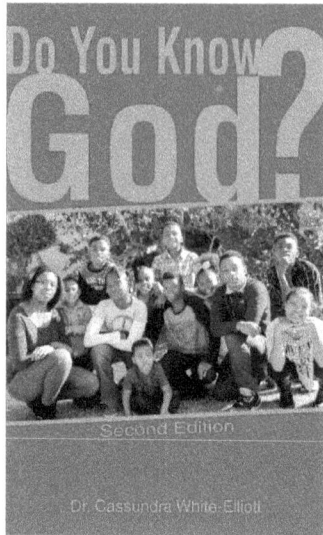

Have you or someone you know ever felt alone, confused, or unsure about your walk with God or are you unsure of what being a Christian is all about? *Do You Know God?* is an excellent text for providing answers to many of your questions. This book introduces adolescents and young adults to God in addition to answer many of their questions about being a Christian. This book shares the testimonies of the trials and tribulations that other teens have experienced and how God prevailed in their lives. All the information that is shared on the pages of the book is based upon the Word of God and the scriptures are taken from the King James Version of the Bible. If you are interested in knowing more about God's Word or how to begin your Christian experience, this book is for you.

Daughter, God Loves You!

"... for her price is far above rubies"
(Proverbs 31:10b)

Dr. Cassundra White-Elliott

Maybe you have heard the proclamation, "The world is going to hell in a hand basket!" Well, I believe I must concur.

However, I do *not* believe, we- the adult, mature believers- should sit idly by and allow our daughters (and our sons for that matter) to go with it! We must fight for our girls and young women, for they are the mothers of tomorrow, and some may even be young mothers today. Not only will they continue the human race, but also they can have bright futures in their careers and as leaders in our society, as they allow God to direct their paths and order their steps.

Daughter, God Loves You! is an earnest attempt to address many of the issues that plague our society and turn our daughters' heads away from God.

In this book, we dive head first into topics such as God's love, the importance and impact of education, the effects of social media, overcoming abuse, and the proper perspective of the future.

For the young adult women- Reading this book will empower you to have a bright prosperous future from being enlightened about the dangers that plague our society and how to avoid pitfalls, as you walk along the path God has paved for you.

I invite all of you to take this journey with me to save our daughters and yourselves (young women) from corruption, by being empowered with knowledge.

We must thwart the plan of the enemy. So, LET'S GO!

CLF Publishing, LLC.
www.clfpublishing.org

ISBN 978-0-9961971-9-9
90000

9 780996 197199

Dr. C. White-Elliott's books are available at:
www.creativemindsbookstore.com
www.amazon.com
www.barnesandnoble.com

Web of Lies

A year ago, Charlito Jimenez was found in his den, lying on the couch, with a fatal gunshot wound in his temple. Everyone in the community still wants to know who is guilty of the unfathomable crime.

Tinisha Salisbury, attorney at law, has taken the case of the accused. Can she prove her client's innocence or will a guilty verdict be rendered?

Halfway through the trial, a badly burned body was found at the scene of a fire.

Is there a string of murders being committed?

Are the murders related?

Web of Lies spins the tales of several characters into one web. Each has a story to tell, and everyone has something to hide. The web of lies, deceit, and revenge take over the lives of these characters to the point where they may not be able to see their way clear.

Embracing Womanhood

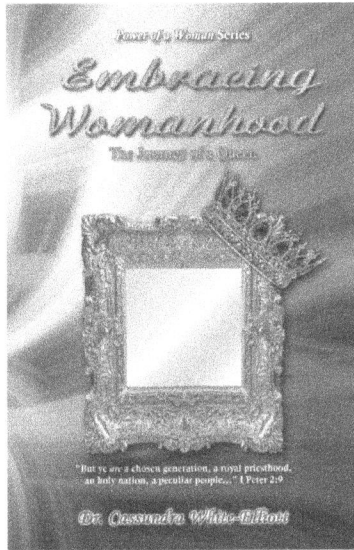

The journey from adolescence through puberty to young adulthood can be challenging and quite disconcerting for the average young lady. The changes that occur both mentally and physically can be both confusing and uncomfortable. However, the outcome of the changes can be beautiful. What she will experience during this time in her life is simply a metamorphosis – taking off the old and embracing the new. The process is similar to that of an awkward caterpillar that overtime develops into a beautiful, graceful butterfly.

The topics covered in this book (puberty, self-esteem, mental stability, goals, finances, and relationships) will assist young women (ages 15–23) in understanding the transformation they are enduring to prepare them for the life that lies ahead. After taking in the information, they will literally witness themselves evolve from princess to queen!

The Making of Dr. C.: A Memoir

The Making of Dr. C. shares the 50-year journey of Dr. Cassundra White-Elliott. Her journey of trials, missteps, successes, and triumphs will inspire you to face any trial you may encounter with a positive attitude and the Word of God.

Her life demonstrates no matter what you may face, there is always a brighter tomorrow.

Keeping the faith will allow God to work in your life. After all, He only wants the best for you!

Prepare for Battle

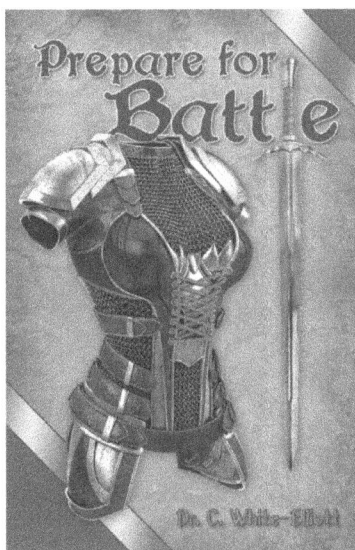

The very life you live is a war zone, riddled with battles ranging from the unexpected to the inconceivable to the paralyzing. The only way for you to successfully navigate through each battle unscathed or with minimal damage or loss is to equip yourself with the full armor of God, which consists of the girdle of truth, the breastplate of righteousness, the gospel of peace, the shield of faith, the helmet of salvation, and the sword of the spirit. To seal your victory, prayer is just as essential a component as each piece of armor. Therefore, the seven aforementioned items serve to comprise the arsenal necessary for winning wars.

This book goes to great lengths to explain each piece of armor in depth, with use of commentaries. The more you understand the importance of the arsenal, its function in battle, and how to effectively use it, the better prepared you will be when unexpected or inconceivable or paralyzing battles confront you.

Equipping yourself today for battle, with the full armor of God, will prevent Satan, our adversary, from annihilating you.

Safety in Him

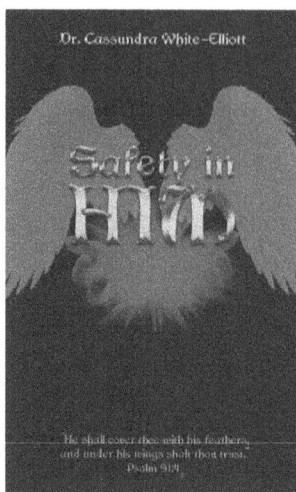

Luke 21:33 declares, *"Heaven and earth shall pass away: but my words shall not pass away,"* and Jeremiah 1:12 says, *"Then said the Lord unto me, Thou hast well seen: for I will hasten my word to perform it."* According to these two verses, we can stand firmly on the Word of God at all times because His Word is everlasting, and He watches over it continuously to perform it.

While the promises of man may go unfulfilled, God's Word is true and He declares, *"So shall my word be that goeth forth out of my mouth: it shall not return unto me void, but it shall accomplish that which I please, and it shall prosper in the thing whereto I sent it"* (Isaiah 55:11).

In this book, particular attention is brought to Psalm 91:1-7. In these verses, God promises His divine protection for His children. Read Christopher's story and see how the divine protective nature of God is demonstrated and remember Acts 10:34b, which states, *"God is no respecter of persons."* What He is able to do for one, He is able to do for another. So, no matter what you be faced with today, call on the Lord, and He will deliver you!

Women's Study Bible

NEW INTERNATIONAL VERSION

Red Letter Bible

CLF PUBLISHING, LLC

Learn the Bible Series

(26 books from A-Z to teach children biblical principles and prominent characters.)
Currently available are A-K. More coming soon!

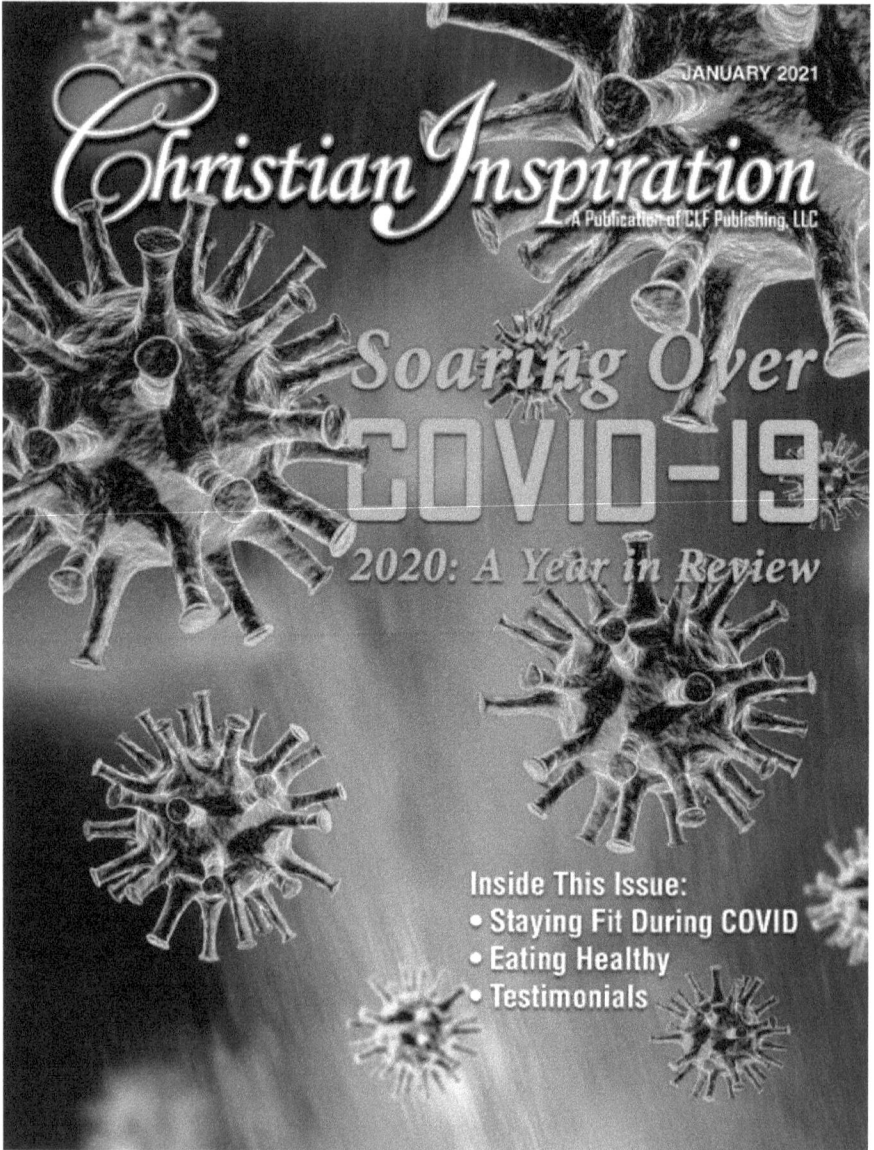

Christian Inspiration is a quarterly magazine with issues released each year in January, April, July, and October. The magazine covers topics germane to Christian living and the world at large.